PLANT IDENTIFIERS

PLANTS FOR
WATER GARDENS

PLANTS FOR
WATER GARDENS

MALCOLM EDWARDS
KENCHESTER WATER GARDENS

DP

DEMPSEY
PARR

This edition first published in 1999 by
Dempsey Parr
Queen Street House
4–5 Queen Street
Bath BA1 1HE

Conceived, edited, illustrated
and produced by Robert Ditchfield Publishers

ISBN 1 84084 338 1

A copy of the British Library Cataloguing in Publication
Data is available from the Library.

Typeset by Action Publishing Technology Ltd, Gloucester
Colour origination by Colour Quest Graphic Services Ltd,
London E9
Printed and bound in Hong Kong

Many of the photographs were taken at the nursery
and water gardens founded by the author:
Kenchester Water Gardens
Church Road
Lyde
Hereford HR1 3AB
Tel: 01432 270981

Half title page: Japanese primulas
Frontispiece: *Iris sibirica* 'Topic Night' and
Hosta fortunei var. *albopicta*
Title page: *Iris laevigata* cultivar
Contents page: *Nymphaea* 'Fabiola'

CONTENTS

INTRODUCTION

TRADITIONALLY WATER GARDENING was the preserve of those gardeners who were fortunate enough to have natural water. With the advent of affordable modern materials to help make structures that could hold water, the pleasures of water gardening became available to all of us. It is now immensely popular and with justification, for almost all gardens are enhanced by the addition of an appropriate water feature.

Most gardeners become fascinated by the diversity of beautiful plants which flourish in an aquatic environment. They realize that aquatic plants enable us to introduce architectural form not seen in many herbaceous and perennial plants. Yet experienced gardeners often reject their hard-earned knowledge of plants, thinking that there is something completely different about the culture of aquatic and moisture-loving varieties. This is incorrect. All the fundamentals of gardening remain the same: the only consideration is the amount of moisture or planting-depth in water that these wonderful additions require.

WATER PLANTS

Water plants are for the most part trouble-free and robust. If a problem exists, it is usually one of control, for, when planted in their natural environment, plants grow lustily due to the optimum growing conditions and

OPPOSITE: A wonderful display of moisture-loving plants at the margins of a pond in early summer.

stability of the environment, and have to compete. This can be turned to advantage by choosing and associating different plants, having taken into account their structure and period of flowering, so that they provide an extremely long season and continuity of interest.

WATER LILIES

The focal point of many planting schemes are the *Nymphaea* or water lilies. The water lily is the specimen plant of the water garden, blooming spectacularly throughout the summer season and providing shade in the pool with its attractive leaf-cover.

Selection of the right water lilies requires care and thought, as these generally robust plants are extremely diverse in size, and a variety that is too large for its environment will quickly lose its appeal as its abundant energy will cause many of its spectacular blooms to be concealed in the ever enlarging canopy of leaves. Due to their rhizomatous nature, some difficulties exist identifying the spread of lilies because they can be greatly influenced by the nutrients available, by the planting depths and by the varieties themselves. Many lilies will naturally grow towards deeper water and in the fullness of time some varieties can accommodate 2.4m to 3m/8ft to 10ft depths. The leaf which is produced on new cuttings of lilies has to reach the surface to enable the cycle of growth to be completed, whilst also producing from the same source of energy in the rhizome the anchorage and feeding roots. A common failure with water lilies is to introduce too quickly cuttings or barely rooted plants to excessive water depths, whereas a mature example of the same plant can

Nymphaea 'Anna Epple'

Nymphaea 'Froebelii'

Nymphaea 'Gold Medal'

Nymphaea 'Gladstoneana'

easily cope with considerably greater depths. In addition the rhizome of the water lily should not be buried underneath the planting medium as this can cause rotting; growing tips should always be exposed.

GROWING OTHER WATER PLANTS

As many aquatic plants are advantageously contained within perforated planting crates (baskets), those varieties which require abundant moisture only during the growing and flowering season and a drier situation during the dormant period can be readily accommodated. The easiest method of dealing with

Late summer and still the margins of the pond are full of interest.

these is to relocate the marginal basket to a garden border area where it can be buried to its rim in soil and a top mulch placed over the crown. Many plants associated with water gardening are of a succulent nature making it necessary to protect them from slugs and snails.

Due to their abundant growth, most moisture plants and nearly all aquatics benefit from the addition of trace elements on a regular basis. An appropriate fertilizer should be applied, but care should be taken not to increase phosphate and nitrate levels which are present in non-aquatic fertilizers. Our own nursery uses a proprietory liquid feed.

THE PLANTS IN THIS BOOK

This book is divided into three sections. The first, arranged in alphabetical order, contains aquatic plants, including water lilies (*Nymphaea*), and examples of deep water aquatics, floating aquatics and oxygenating plants.

Deep water aquatics are plants which grow with the crown well below the water surface but with leaves and flowers at or above the surface. Plant these at a water depth of 15–45cm/6in–$1^1/_2$ft, treating them like a shallow water lily.

Floating aquatics are plants which drift with the current, providing shade and serving as a larder for many natural fish food such as fly eggs and larvae. Most attractive species are often tender and require winter protection indoors.

Oxygenating plants are plants which by their vigorous growth reduce the level of dissolved pollutants (nitrates) whilst, during the hours of sunlight, they take in carbon dioxide and give off oxygen. They are the pond's workers and need to be introduced in large quantities for beneficial effect. Their growth is predominantly below the water surface.

The second section of the book contains **marginal plants**, which grow with the crown of the plant at or below the water surface.

The third section contains **moisture-loving plants** to plant in moist beds at the pool side. The crown should be above the water line at all times, though some of these plants may thrive with their root systems in the pool, whilst others will die unless they have well-drained soil.

Approximate measurements of a plant's height and spread (or spread only or height only, where appropriate) are given in both metric and imperial measures. If two measurements are given, the height is the first measurement, as in for example 1.2m × 60cm/4 × 2ft. However, both height and spread vary so greatly from garden to garden since they depend on soil, climate, pruning and position, that these measurements are offered as guides only.

Planting depth: this is given where relevant in the case of aquatic and marginal plants.

The following symbols are also used:

= Example of symbol of growth for water lilies: this is given to indicate the size of the plant at the surface in an area either 1m/3ft square or 2m/6ft square.

○   = the plant thrives in or tolerates full sun.

◑   = thrives in or tolerates part-shade.

●   = thrives in or tolerates full shade.

E   = the plant is evergreen.

LH   = needs acid soil and is intolerant of lime.

❄❄❄   = the plant is fully hardy and can survive winters in temperate regions.

❄❄   = the plant is only frost-hardy, not fully hardy and it is likely it will need shelter and protection during winter in temperate regions.

✳ = the plant is tender (or half-hardy) and even in mild winter areas it may need protection to survive, or can be grown under glass.

GLOSSARY

Rhizome An underground stem, which creeps but has the same storage purpose as a bulb or tuber.

Sinus The cleft in a water lily leaf, for example, at the entrance to the stem.

Spadix A flowering spike, normally thick and fleshy, with a number of small flowers. This is typically found in the arum family.

Stellate Arranged like a star, a characteristic of many water lily blooms.

POISONOUS PLANTS

In recent years, concern has been voiced about poisonous plants or plants which can cause allergic reactions if touched. The fact is that many plants are poisonous, some in a particular part, others in all their parts. For the sake of safety, it is always, without exception, essential to assume that no part of a plant should be eaten unless it is known, without any doubt whatsoever, that the plant or its part is edible and that it cannot provoke an allergic reaction in the individual person who samples it. It must also be remembered that some plants can cause severe dermatitis, blistering or an allergic reaction if touched, in some individuals and not in others. It is the responsibility of the individual to take all the above into account.

WATER IN THE GARDEN

All water gardens are beautiful, but sadly they can be dangerous, mostly to children who can drown in even a few inches of water, or sometimes to adults. We would urge readers where necessary to take account of this and provide a reliable means of protection if they include water in the garden.

1.
AQUATIC PLANTS

This wonderful deep marginal variety develops from a tuber. The submerged stems reach the water surface and develop an elongated spear-shaped leaf in an attractive mid-green. Older leaves frequently develop dark burgundy blotches. The prolific sweetly scented blooms have a hawthorn perfume arising from the snowy white flowers with black anthers. Blooms occasionally appear with a slight pink blush.

Height: Leaves lie on the surface of the pool with flowers proud of the surface.

Position: Up to 45cm/1½ft in water depth, best in sun but will tolerate part shade.

Care: Propagation by viable seed produced or division of tuberous rhizomes. Seedlings will often appear at the water margins.

◯◑　✻✻✻

Containing globular floating sacks of air-filled tissue with the shell-shaped glaucous green leaf, this tropical plant is extremely vigorous and expands by the production of runners which form plantlets at the tip. It is grown for the spectacular hyacinth flower in lilac/pink. It is not hardy – the frost will kill it – so it is a seasonal introduction to most pool situations and should be treated as an annual. It flowers for most of the summer.

Height: Up to 30cm/1ft.

Position: Floating plant needing a position in full sun.

Care: Introduce to outside pools after all danger of frost is past. Either discard in winter or place young plants in water in a frost-free glasshouse. Propagate by separating off young plantlets.

| ○ | ❄ |

Lagarosiphon major (syn. *Elodea crispa*)

This is one of the most vigorous and recommended submerged oxygenating plants with densely clothed stems of tightly reflected leaves along its length. Its branching habit is encouraged by nipping out the rosette shaped tips. For pond use this encourages dense lower growth which is to be preferred to the extremely long individual stems which can result if not pruned.

Height: Up to 3ft/1m submerged stems. Their spread is indefinite.

Position: Submerged oxygenator which will thrive best in ponds exposed to full sun.

Care: Propagation by division. Prune as necessary to prevent the pond from becoming overcrowded.

| ◯ | Semi-E | ❄❄❄ |

Nuphar lutea: Brandy bottle

The submerged leaf form is waxy, soft, vegetative in a pale green. Emergent foliage is water lily-like in habit, floating on the surface of the water. The oval, mid to dark green leaf is up to 30 × 25cm/12 × 10in and very tough. The flower stands close to the surface and is yellow. This variety will tolerate slowly flowing water. Flowers throughout the summer.

Height: Floats on the surface of the pool. Individual plant spread is 1.5m/5ft.

Position: Best in water that is at least 1m/3ft deep and will naturalize in 3m/10ft deep water.

Care: Propagate by division of rhizome.

◯ ◑ | ✳✳✳

Nymphaea 'Amabalis': Water lily

Young leaves emerge with the upper surface reddish-hued, maturing to a mid-green with evident veining. The crisply stellate flower is a pleasing pink around the yellow stamens, blushing out to almost white at the outer petals. The leaf is round with a wide open sinus (cleft at the entrance to the stem) and is 23cm/9in in diameter. The large bloom can attain 18cm/7in.

Planting depth: 60cm/2ft

Spread: 2m/6ft

Care: Provide fertile soil, full sun and avoid water splash. Divide congested plants. Generally water lilies are trouble-free but remove water lily beetles, aphids and plants affected with crown rot.

19

Nymphaea 'American Star': Water lily

A rich pink stellate lily with narrow petals, fading towards the tips. Not prolific in bloom, this attractive 15cm/6in flower is worth the wait. The large leaf size makes this a better choice for the bigger pool where the undisturbed rhizome is permitted to create large colonies. This will improve the ratio of flower to leaf produced.

Planting depth: 60cm/2ft

Spread: 1.5m/5ft

Care: Provide fertile soil, full sun and avoid water splash. Divide congested plants. Generally water lilies are trouble-free but remove water lily beetles, aphids and plants affected with crown rot.

2m/6ft
2m/6ft

○ | ✳✳✳

This fine lily is recommended for medium to larger ponds.
It produces a large open heavily petalled bloom of
18cm/7in diameter, of the palest blush-pink with a
distinctive yellow centre. The new leaf is shaded slightly
with burgundy but matures to a mid-green on the upper
surface, with a light copper underside. The leaf has a
diameter of 25cm/10in.

Planting depth: 75cm/2¹⁄₂ft

Spread: 2m/6ft

Care: Provide fertile soil, full sun and avoid water
splash. Divide congested plants. Generally water lilies
are trouble-free but remove water lily beetles, aphids and
plants affected with crown rot.

○ ❄❄❄

This lily is remarkable for its variously shaded, mottled and blotched leaf colour. The olive background to the leaf bears shades of red, cream, pale yellow, and pink blotches. The 23cm/9in diameter leaf is immediately identifiable in any planting. The flower is composed of slim petals with a fairly open cup shape of a faint pink blush which is totally overpowered by the foliage.

Planting depth: 60–75cm/2–2¹/₂ft

Spread: 1.5m/5ft

Care: Provide fertile soil, full sun and avoid water splash. Divide congested plants. Generally water lilies are trouble-free but remove water lily beetles, aphids and plants affected with crown rot.

☽ ❄❄❄

A really striking, deep dark-red bloom of 18cm/7in diameter, with dark stamens tipped with anthers of deep yellow, is freely produced and combines brilliantly on this water lily with the new leaf colour, which appears as a deep mahogany shade changing to a crisp green with maturity. The leaves have a diameter of 23cm/9in and a wide open sinus.

Planting depth: Up to 75cm/2¹/₂ft

Spread: 1.2m/4ft

Care: Provide fertile soil, full sun and avoid water splash. Divide congested plants. Generally water lilies are trouble-free but remove water lily beetles, aphids and plants affected with crown rot.

2m/6ft

2m/6ft

○ ❄❄❄

Nymphaea 'Attraction': Water lily

The striking red bloom on this variety is up to 20cm/8in in diameter. It is freely produced and is reliable. With the new leaf having a bronzed underside, mature leaves, which are about 25cm/10in in diameter, are a pleasing green. The sinus overlaps. Due to its vigorous nature this is an excellent choice for medium and large pools.

Planting depth: Up to 75cm/2½ft

Spread: 1.5m/5ft

Care: Provide fertile soil, full sun and avoid water splash. Divide congested plants. Generally water lilies are trouble-free but remove water lily beetles, aphids and plants affected with crown rot.

24

This is an absolutely stunning bloom of the darkest red, which has the appearance of rich velvet. Produced prolifically, these striking blooms are 12.5cm/5in in diameter and have burnt orange stamens, tipped with yellow centres, over an emergent leaf of green tinged with burgundy, maturing to green faintly retaining a burgundy edge. It has an open sinus and the leaf is 20cm/8in in diameter.

Planting depth: 60cm/2ft

Spread: 1.2m/4ft

Care: Provide fertile soil, full sun and avoid water splash. Divide congested plants. Generally water lilies are trouble-free but remove water lily beetles, aphids and plants affected with crown rot.

○ ❋❋❋

25

Nymphaea 'Brakeleyi Rosea': Water lily

A long established variety of water lily, less prolific in bloom than many of the new introductions. It is suited to medium to large-sized pools where its spreading rhizome will create an expanding colony. The soft stellate pale pink flowers with yellow centres are sweetly scented. The new leaves emerge in a burgundy shade and gradually turn green as they mature when they attain 25cm/10in in diameter.

Planting depth: Up to 75cm/2¹/₂ft

Spread: 1.5m/5ft

Care: Provide fertile soil, full sun and avoid water splash. Divide congested plants. Generally water lilies are trouble-free but remove water lily beetles, aphids and plants affected with crown rot.

Nymphaea **'Cactus Pink'**: Water lily

The very open, slim, lance-shaped petals of this variety which are frequently held above the surface of the pond, show a loose stellate formation that makes it particularly appealing. With a diameter of 18cm/7in, the round green mature leaf makes the spectacular flower appear larger than its actual 12.5cm/5in size.

Planting depth: 60cm/2ft

Spread: 1.2m/4ft

Care: Provide fertile soil, full sun and avoid water splash. Divide congested plants. Generally water lilies are trouble-free but remove water lily beetles, aphids and plants affected with crown rot.

2m/6ft

2m/6ft

◯ ❋❋❋

This pink lily deserves its popularity. It is very free flowering with a profusion of 12.5cm/5in diameter pale pink blooms. The new leaf is an attractive purple on the upper surface and a dusky red on the underside. In maturity the leaves attain 20cm/8in in diameter and become green, with an open sinus (cleft at the entrance to the stem).

Planting depth: 75cm/2½ft

Spread: 1.5m/5ft

Care: Provide fertile soil, full sun and avoid water splash. Divide congested plants. Generally water lilies are trouble-free but remove water lily beetles, aphids and plants affected with crown rot.

○ ❊❊❊

Nymphaea 'Caroliniana Nivea': Water lily

The stellate 15cm/6in flowers of creamy white have a yellow centre and a beautiful perfume. The leaf is almost rounded and light green both on the top and undersides. It is 25cm/10in in diameter making this lily one for the larger pool. The blooms increase as the colonizing rhizome expands and, given the right opportunity, will gradually form a very large group.

Planting depth: 75cm/2¹/₂ft

Spread: 1.5m/5ft

Care: Provide fertile soil, full sun and avoid water splash. Divide congested plants. Generally water lilies are trouble-free but remove water lily beetles, aphids and plants affected with crown rot.

Nymphaea 'Caroliniana Perfecta': Water lily

This variety has a cup-shaped flower of pink with a slight orange tinge and a bright yellow centre. It is 15cm/6in in diameter and has a sweet smell. The 25cm/10in leaf is heavily veined on the upper surface with a burgundy underside and a holly green topside. The flowering is not prolific on newly established plants but increases with maturity.

Planting depth: 60cm/2ft

Spread: 1.2m/4ft

Care: Provide fertile soil, full sun and avoid water splash. Divide congested plants. Generally water lilies are trouble-free but remove water lily beetles, aphids and plants affected with crown rot.

The beautiful large yellow bloom develops a peach blush as it matures. The 18cm/7in blooms are fragrant and cup-shaped. The leaf is green, large and shows attractive heavy purple blotches. The leaf sinus is an open 'V'. This variety is not readily available but it is well worth searching for at specialist suppliers.

Planting depth: 75cm/2½ft

Spread: 1.5m/5ft

Care: Provide fertile soil, full sun and avoid water splash. Divide congested plants. Generally water lilies are trouble-free but remove water lily beetles, aphids and plants affected with crown rot.

2m/6ft

2m/6ft

◐ ❀❀❀

Nymphaea 'Charlene Strawn': Water lily

The pleasing mid-green 23cm/9in leaf shows the characteristic of yellow lilies with its light purple mottling. The flower is a really attractive yellow with a golden centre and its stellate form makes the large blooms of 20cm/8in in diameter very appealing. It is ideally suited to pools where surface cover is desired, as it is prolific in leaf.

Planting depth: 75cm/2¹/₂ft

Spread: 1.5m/5ft

Care: Provide fertile soil, full sun and avoid water splash. Divide congested plants. Generally water lilies are trouble-free but remove water lily beetles, aphids and plants affected with crown rot.

2m/6ft

2m/6ft

○ ❊❊❊

Nymphaea 'Charles de Meurville': Water lily

This stellate flower with deep carmine inner petals and paler pink outside petals has a bright orange centre and is 18cm/7in diameter. The long oval leaf is dark green, the underside being distinctly veined and the sinus is an elongated 'V'. The leaf can attain sizes of up to 25cm × 20cm/10in × 8in. This prolific lily is an ideal choice for medium or large pools.

Planting depth: 60cm/2ft

Spread: 1.5m/5ft

Care: Provide fertile soil, full sun and avoid water splash. Divide congested plants. Generally water lilies are trouble-free but remove water lily beetles, aphids and plants affected with crown rot.

2m/6ft

☾ ❄❄❄

33

Nymphaea 'Comanche': Water lily

With maturing 12.5cm/5in flowers ranging from predominantly yellow when first opening, through yellow with a golden centre, through gold to almost orange, this plant makes identification confusing. Even the shape of the flower changes with maturity from cup-like to stellate. It is highly desirable for small to medium pools. The 25cm/10in leaves are characteristically flecked with purple.

Planting depth: 60cm/2ft

Spread: 1.2m/4ft

Care: Provide fertile soil, full sun and avoid water splash. Divide congested plants. Generally water lilies are trouble-free but remove water lily beetles, aphids and plants affected with crown rot.

2m/6ft

2m/6ft

○ | ❄❄❄

This striking pink lily, of stellate form, has a deepening colour in maturity on the outside petals. The flowers open to a diameter of 12.5cm/5in and are held over green leaves which display a very light veining on their upper surface, whilst the under surface which is heavily veined is of a dark burgundy. The leaf grows to 12.5cm/5in in diameter and has an open sinus.

Planting depth: Up to 60cm/2ft

Spread: 1m/3ft

Care: Provide fertile soil, full sun and avoid water splash. Divide congested plants. Generally water lilies are trouble-free but remove water lily beetles, aphids and plants affected with crown rot.

○ ❄❄❄

Nymphaea 'Darwin': Water lily

This free-flowering large pink lily is a particular favourite. Its impressive 18cm/7in, almost double-petalled blooms shade from a pleasing pink to a white-flushed pink at the outside and are often held slightly above the surface. The combination of these flowers with the young leaves produced in a mahogany colour, maturing to a pleasing mid-green, makes it suitable for any medium to large pool.

Planting depth: 75cm/2¹/₂ft

Spread: 1.5m/5ft

Care: Provide fertile soil, full sun and avoid water splash. Divide congested plants. Generally water lilies are trouble-free but remove water lily beetles, aphids and plants affected with crown rot.

2m/6ft

2m/6ft

◐ ❄❄❄

Nymphaea 'Ellisiana': Water lily

With its small, brilliant red blooms, and its 18cm/7in diameter leaves, this is an ideal selection for small pond or tub culture. This lily is one of the less vigorous varieties which makes it an especial choice for contained areas, as it has a tendency to concentrate its energies on producing an abundance of 10cm/4in diameter blooms.

Planting depth: 45–60cm/1¹/₂–2ft

Spread: 1m/3ft

Care: Provide fertile soil, full sun and avoid water splash. Divide congested plants. Generally water lilies are trouble-free but remove water lily beetles, aphids and plants affected with crown rot.

○ ✳✳✳

Nymphaea 'Fabiola' (formerly 'Mrs Richmond'): Water lily

With its broad petals of a pleasing deep pink at the centre, shading out through light pink to almost white at the outside, the 15cm/6in diameter flowers which are produced in profusion, make this a wonderful selection for a medium-sized pool. The new leaf is burgundy quickly changing to mid-green, 28cm/11in in diameter with an overlapping sinus.

Planting depth: Up to 75cm/2½ft

Spread: 1.5m/5ft

Care: Provide fertile soil, full sun and avoid water splash. Divide congested plants. Generally water lilies are trouble-free but remove water lily beetles, aphids and plants affected with crown rot.

○ ❋❋❋

Nymphaea 'Formosa': Water lily

The bloom of this delightful pink lily is pale pink on the outer petals, deeper pink towards the centre; all petals bearing wildly differing degrees of white flecking. This effect almost gives the appearance of different blooms. The 20cm/8in diameter leaf is olive green on the upper surface with a reddish tinge to the underside of the leaf.

Planting depth: 60cm/2ft

Spread: 1.2m/4ft

Care: Provide fertile soil, full sun and avoid water splash. Divide congested plants. Generally water lilies are trouble-free but remove water lily beetles, aphids and plants affected with crown rot.

2m/6ft

2m/6ft

◑ ❄❄❄

Nymphaea **'Froebelii'**: Water lily

This variety carries many pleasing dark wine-red flowers
of about 10cm/4in in diameter. The flower has a distinctly
square appearance inside with red stamens. The leaves are
mid-green, slightly marbled and reddish at their margins.
They are approximately 15cm/6in in size with an open
sinus. This is a very suitable cultivar for small ponds and
a prolific bloomer.

Planting depth: 45–60cm/1½–2ft

Spread: 1m/3ft

Care: Provide fertile soil, full sun and avoid water
splash. Divide congested plants. Generally water lilies
are trouble-free but remove water lily beetles, aphids and
plants affected with crown rot.

○ ❋❋❋

Nymphaea **'Gladstoneana'**: Water lily

The new leaf is bronzed, maturing to green, but retaining the bronze colour underneath. There is visible veining to the upper leaf and it is very large at 30cm/12in diameter. The pleasant white bloom may appear dwarfed by the large leaf but at 15cm/6in in diameter it is a good selection for the larger water garden because of its vigour.

Planting depth: 1m/3ft

Spread: 2m/6ft

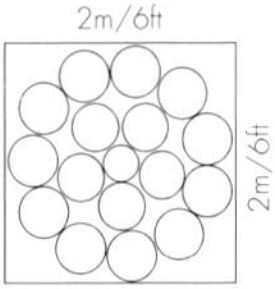

Care: Provide fertile soil, full sun and avoid water splash. Divide congested plants. Generally water lilies are trouble-free but remove water lily beetles, aphids and plants affected with crown rot.

2m/6ft

2m/6ft

| ◯ | �֍ �֍ �֍ |

Nymphaea 'Gold Medal': Water lily

This lovely, heavily petalled yellow-flowered cultivar has all of the best characteristics of a quality water lily – prolific in bloom, with an attractive dark olive-green upper leaf surface with purple mottling. The flower size is up to 18cm/7in in diameter with leaves of 25cm/10in in diameter. Here is a lily that is recommended for medium or large pools.

Planting depth: 75cm/2½ft

Spread: 1.5m/5ft

Care: Provide fertile soil, full sun and avoid water splash. Divide congested plants. Generally water lilies are trouble-free but remove water lily beetles, aphids and plants affected with crown rot.

Nymphaea 'Gonnère': Water lily

This is one of the finest white lilies for any pool. The impressive 10–12cm/4–5in double white blooms are open longer in the day and form a spectacular globe with a distinctive yellow centre, which is slightly perfumed on first opening. The new leaves are bronze, maturing to a uniform green. The round leaf has an open sinus and is 20cm/8in in diameter.

Planting depth: 60cm/2ft

Spread: 1m/3ft

Care: Provide fertile soil, full sun and avoid water splash. Divide congested plants. Generally water lilies are trouble-free but remove water lily beetles, aphids and plants affected with crown rot.

Nymphaea 'Hermine': Water lily

The heart-shaped leaves with their open sinus are slightly bronze when new but turn to dusky green on maturity. The single star-shaped flowers of white with their yellow centre have a simple charm. The flowers are 12.5cm/5in in diameter while the leaves achieve 18cm/7in across. This lily is highly suitable for small ponds or for tub culture.

Planting depth: Up to 45cm/1½ft

Spread: Up to 75cm/2½ft

Care: Provide fertile soil, full sun and avoid water splash. Divide congested plants. Generally water lilies are trouble-free but remove water lily beetles, aphids and plants affected with crown rot.

○ | ❋❋❋

Nymphaea 'James Brydon': Water lily

This is one of the most popular red water lilies. Its 12.5cm/5in flower, in a gay 'hunting pink' colour with a bright reddish-orange centre, is cup-shaped and pleasantly fragranced. The 18cm/7in leaves are burgundy coloured when they emerge but they mature to a uniform green with a closed sinus. It is very prolific and suits most situations.

Planting depth: 60cm/2ft

Spread: 1.2m/4ft

Care: Provide fertile soil, full sun and avoid water splash. Divide congested plants. Generally water lilies are trouble-free but remove water lily beetles, aphids and plants affected with crown rot.

2m/6ft

2m/6ft

⟨○⟩ ❄❄❄

Nymphaea **'Madame Wilfon Gonnère'**: Water lily

If a single pink lily is going to be selected for a planting scheme, this has to be one of the first for consideration. With a rich pink centre fading out to a lighter pink on the outside, heavy petalled double blooms of 12.5cm/5in in diameter are held over an attractive plain green 23cm/9in diameter leaf. This is the choice for any pond.

Planting depth: 60cm/2ft

Spread: 1.2m/4ft

Care: Provide fertile soil, full sun and avoid water splash. Divide congested plants. Generally water lilies are trouble-free but remove water lily beetles, aphids and plants affected with crown rot.

○ | ❄❄❄

Nymphaea 'Mayla': Water lily

The new leaves appear in a pleasing reddish-burgundy shade and as they mature, although still showing evidence of this burgundy shading until maturity, develop into a uniform mid-green with a closed sinus, but remain maroon on the underside. Flowers are of a strong pink blush and are 10cm/4in in diameter with a burnt orange centre.

Planting depth: 60cm/2ft

Spread: 1.2m/4ft

Care: Provide fertile soil, full sun and avoid water splash. Divide congested plants. Generally water lilies are trouble-free but remove water lily beetles, aphids and plants affected with crown rot.

Nymphaea 'Météor': Water lily

The centre petals of this very free-flowering variety are a pleasing red with the outer petals shading to pink showing white at the tips, this variation resulting in an attractive bloom of about 15cm/6in in diameter. The leaves appear distinctly bronze, and with maturity will attain a diameter of 23cm/9in by which time they will have changed to a uniform green.

Planting depth: 60cm/2ft

Spread: 1.5m/5ft

Care: Provide fertile soil, full sun and avoid water splash. Divide congested plants. Generally water lilies are trouble-free but remove water lily beetles, aphids and plants affected with crown rot.

☽ ❋❋❋

Nymphaea odorata var. *minor*: Water lily

This dainty lily bears pure white fragrant flowers of
5cm/2in in diameter and the small 12.5cm/5in leaves,
which are green on the upper surface and mahogany
underside, make it an ideal selection for tub culture and
the smallest pools. Prolific in bloom, it will reproduce by
the production of naturally occurring seedlings when
conditions are suitable.

Planting depth: Up to 45cm/1¹/₂ft

Spread: 60cm/2ft

Care: Provide fertile soil, full sun and avoid water
splash. Divide congested plants. Generally water lilies
are trouble-free but remove water lily beetles, aphids and
plants affected with crown rot.

○ ❄❄❄

49

Nymphaea 'Odorata Sulphurea': Water lily

The 20cm/8in open bloom with its distinctive yellow petals and brighter yellow centre makes this variety a cheerful water lily. The new leaves are light green, mottled burgundy on the upper side, the underside being rather more heavily mottled burgundy. The 25cm/10in leaves are nearly round and the sinus is 'V' shaped. As the name suggests, new blooms are scented.

Planting depth: 60cm/2ft

Spread: 1.2m/4ft

Care: Provide fertile soil, full sun and avoid water splash. Divide congested plants. Generally water lilies are trouble-free but remove water lily beetles, aphids and plants affected with crown rot.

2m/6ft

2m/6ft

◯ ✳✳✳

Nymphaea 'Odorata Turicensis': Water lily

Pleasantly fragrant, this has a flower which is the palest soft blush of pink with a golden yellow centre. This bloom which can attain a diameter of 15cm/6in is stellate in form and the leaf has a green upper surface with a bronze underside. The sinus is open and the leaf size is 15cm/6in across. It is well suited to the small/medium pool.

Planting depth: Up to 60cm/2ft

Spread: 75cm/2¹/₂ft

Care: Provide fertile soil, full sun and avoid water splash. Divide congested plants. Generally water lilies are trouble-free but remove water lily beetles, aphids and plants affected with crown rot.

○ ❋❋❋

Nymphaea 'Paul Hariot': Water lily

This lily is normally listed under the category of Variables. When it opens, it displays outer petals which are orange suffused with pink which shade to peach pink. Later it progresses through a variety of shades. When fully established it is difficult to identify without a close examination. The flowers are 10cm/4in across and the 15cm/6in leaves are green with mahogany blotches.

Planting depth: 60cm/2ft

Spread: 1m/3ft

Care: Provide fertile soil, full sun and avoid water splash. Divide congested plants. Generally water lilies are trouble-free but remove water lily beetles, aphids and plants affected with crown rot.

◑ ❄❄❄

Nymphaea **Pearl of the Pool**: Water lily

With maturity the spreading rhizome permits the production of increasing numbers of the fragrant, striking pink 15cm/6in diameter stellate blooms of this lily. New leaves emerge in a pleasing burgundy shade, becoming green with maturity. The round fully mature leaf can attain 25cm/10in in diameter and has a closed sinus, with its leaf edges sometimes overlapping.

Planting depth: Up to 75cm/2¹/₂ft

Spread: 1.5m/5ft

Care: Provide fertile soil, full sun and avoid water splash. Divide congested plants. Generally water lilies are trouble-free but remove water lily beetles, aphids and plants affected with crown rot.

○ ❄❄❄

The 23cm/9in leaf is a uniform green having emerged in a damson shade, whilst the underside remains red. It has light veining and a sinus in the form of a 'V'. The 12.5cm/5in flower is stellate shaped with pretty pink crinkled petals (as the name suggests) and a deep yellow centre. This lily is very happy in small, medium or large pools.

Planting depth: 60cm/2ft

Spread: 1.2m/4ft

Care: Provide fertile soil, full sun and avoid water splash. Divide congested plants. Generally water lilies are trouble-free but remove water lily beetles, aphids and plants affected with crown rot.

Nymphaea 'Perry's Double White': Water lily

The heavy petalling of the double white bloom is beautifully complemented by the golden centre of this variety. The stellate form of crisp white flower combined with the deep green upper surface to the 20cm/8in diameter leaves makes this stand out as a suitable selection for any pool. With a flower size of 15cm/6in diameter, it emits a fragrance which is apparent on first opening.

Planting depth: 60cm/2ft

Spread: 1.2m/4ft

Care: Provide fertile soil, full sun and avoid water splash. Divide congested plants. Generally water lilies are trouble-free but remove water lily beetles, aphids and plants affected with crown rot.

With its small brilliant red petals and its deep orange-red centre, the 10cm/4in bloom of this lily is presented as an open cup shape. The attractive leaf appears bronze at first, changing to a uniform green, and is round, 15cm/6in in diameter and has an open sinus. The pleasing combination of flower and leaf makes this variety ideally suited to small ponds.

Planting depth: Up to 60cm/2ft

Spread: 1m/3ft

Care: Provide fertile soil, full sun and avoid water splash. Divide congested plants. Generally water lilies are trouble-free but remove water lily beetles, aphids and plants affected with crown rot.

☽ ❅❅❅

Nymphaea 'Perry's Pink Beauty': Water lily

With their large golden yellow centres the cup-like blooms in light blush pink are pleasantly fragranced on first emerging and are up to 12.5cm/5in in diameter. The rounded leaves are 20cm/8in across and have a closed sinus, the leaves emerging first as a claret-like brown before maturing to mid-green.

Planting depth: Up to 75cm/2¹/₂ft

Spread: 1.5m/5ft

Care: Provide fertile soil, full sun and avoid water splash. Divide congested plants. Generally water lilies are trouble-free but remove water lily beetles, aphids and plants affected with crown rot.

◐ ✳✳✳

Small 10cm/4in stellate flowers of a very deep red with a deep red centre and slim lance-shaped petals distinguish this variety. Though its new leaves are of a purplish shade, they change to green with maturity. These leaves are almost pointed with a wide open sinus and are 15cm/6in in diameter. This is a very good selection for the small/medium pond.

Planting depth: 60cm/2ft

Spread: 1m/3ft

Care: Provide fertile soil, full sun and avoid water splash. Divide congested plants. Generally water lilies are trouble-free but remove water lily beetles, aphids and plants affected with crown rot.

◑ ❋❋❋

Nymphaea 'Perry's Red Star': Water lily

When the new leaf appears, the upper surface is uniformly purple but it changes to green with maturity and is 18cm/7in in diameter. The underside of the leaf is reddish-brown. The striking red bloom is stellate, up to 12.5cm/5in in diameter, and has a dark orange-red centre. This plant has been known to produce viviparously (producing its own plantlets).

Planting depth: 60cm/2ft

Spread: 1.2m/4ft

Care: Provide fertile soil, full sun and avoid water splash. Divide congested plants. Generally water lilies are trouble-free but remove water lily beetles, aphids and plants affected with crown rot.

2m/6ft

O ❉❉❉

A fine variety with a flower of rich rose pink, 18cm/7in in size, which emits a very slight but pleasant fragrance. The combination of the blooms and the mature leaves of a uniform green, with new leaves being produced in reddish brown, makes this lily a most attractive selection for a medium-sized pool. The leaves are up to 25cm/10in in diameter.

Planting depth: 60cm/2ft

Spread: 1.2m/4ft

Care: Provide fertile soil, full sun and avoid water splash. Divide congested plants. Generally water lilies are trouble-free but remove water lily beetles, aphids and plants affected with crown rot.

○ ❄❄❄

Nymphaea 'Perry's Viviparous Pink': Water lily

As the name suggests, this plant will occasionally produce viviparously new plantlets from the spent flower. The bloom is a most attractive open stellate shape, of a glowing rich pink with an orange/yellow centre, 18cm/7in diameter in size. It is held above a large round green leaf, 25cm/10in across, which when first produced is of a rich mahogany shade.

Planting depth: Up to 75cm/2½ft

Spread: 1.5m/5ft

Care: Provide fertile soil, full sun and avoid water splash. Divide congested plants. Generally water lilies are trouble-free but remove water lily beetles, aphids and plants affected with crown rot.

⊙ | ❄❄❄

61

Nymphaea 'Perry's White Star': Water lily

With its large, long, narrow petals, this 15cm/6in wide snowy white lily holds its head above the surface. Its 20cm/8in diameter leaf appears with a mahogany upper surface and a reddish underside, but in maturity the upper side changes to a uniform green. This variety is impressive when the rhizome is permitted to expand, aiding the production of the spectacular blooms.

Planting depth: 60cm/2ft

Spread: 1.2m/4ft

2m/6ft
2m/6ft

Care: Provide fertile soil, full sun and avoid water splash. Divide congested plants. Generally water lilies are trouble-free but remove water lily beetles, aphids and plants affected with crown rot.

◑ ❄❄❄

The round 20cm/8in leaves emerge burgundy, shading to green on maturity and have an almost closed sinus. The 18cm/7in flowers are a delicate pink with yellowish orange centres. The petals are slightly deeper in the centre and paler towards the tips and curve inwards. If allowed to naturalize, the resulting colony will produce flowers very freely.

Planting depth: 60cm/2ft

Spread: 1m/3ft

Care: Provide fertile soil, full sun and avoid water splash. Divide congested plants. Generally water lilies are trouble-free but remove water lily beetles, aphids and plants affected with crown rot.

Nymphaea **'Pink Sensation'**: Water lily

This lily bears a 12.5cm/5in strong pink stellate bloom
with golden anthers. It is justifiably a most popular choice
among the pink water lilies. The new leaves are suffused
with a burgundy flush, changing with maturity to green,
and have an open sinus and are 23cm/9in in size. This
cultivar keeps its flower fully open until much later in the
day than other comparable lilies.

Planting depth: 60cm/2ft

Spread: 1.2m/4ft

Care: Provide fertile soil, full sun and avoid water
splash. Divide congested plants. Generally water lilies
are trouble-free but remove water lily beetles, aphids and
plants affected with crown rot.

2m/6ft

2m/6ft

○ ❄❄❄

Nymphaea 'Queen of the Whites': Water lily

With its ability to provide foliage cover over a considerable area, this lily is ideal for medium to large pools. Its fresh green leaves, shaded burgundy beneath, are large, attaining up to 28cm/11in in size. They are complemented by the fine blooms which are produced in abundance, 18cm/7in across, with crisp white petals and a golden centre.

Planting depth: 75cm/2½ft

Spread: 2m/6ft

Care: Provide fertile soil, full sun and avoid water splash. Divide congested plants. Generally water lilies are trouble-free but remove water lily beetles, aphids and plants affected with crown rot.

2m/6ft

2m/6ft

◯ ❄❄❄

Nymphaea 'Ray Davies': Water lily

The new leaves are produced in an attractive mahogany shade, changing in maturity to mid-green, with a slightly overlapping sinus and attaining 25cm/10in in diameter. The attractive large flowers are 18cm/7in in diameter with shell pink petals and a yellow centre and have a slight but discernible perfume. This is one of the best lilies for the large pool.

Planting depth: 75cm/2¹/₂ft

Spread: 1.5m/5ft

Care: Provide fertile soil, full sun and avoid water splash. Divide congested plants. Generally water lilies are trouble-free but remove water lily beetles, aphids and plants affected with crown rot.

○ ❋❋❋

Nymphaea 'Red Blaze': Water lily

Although this lily does not produce a prolific amount of flowers, their pointed petals and vivid crimson colouring with a bright gold centre make it worthy of recommendation for planting in medium-sized pools. The bloom which bears a very slight fragrance is 12–15cm/5–6in across. The leaf, 20cm/8in in diameter, is a uniform green in maturity, although when new is of a dark burgundy. The sinus is an open 'V'.

Planting depth: 60cm/2ft

Spread: 1.2m/4ft

Care: Provide fertile soil, full sun and avoid water splash. Divide congested plants. Generally water lilies are trouble-free but remove water lily beetles, aphids and plants affected with crown rot.

○ | ❊❊❊

This wonderful new introduction has a striking stellate rich red bloom 12.5cm/5in in diameter with a burnt orange centre and its outer petals flecked with white. The mid-green 15cm/6in sized leaf has an open sinus. It is a superb selection for a medium pool, because of its characteristic ability to flower prolifically and because of its modest leaf-size.

Planting depth: 60cm/2ft

Spread: 1.2m/4ft

Care: Provide fertile soil, full sun and avoid water splash. Divide congested plants. Generally water lilies are trouble-free but remove water lily beetles, aphids and plants affected with crown rot.

○ ✳✳✳

Nymphaea 'René Gérard': Water lily

The new leaf appears in a bronze green changing to uniform green on the upper and lower surfaces. The leaf is up to 25cm/10in in diameter, rounded and the sinus is an open 'V'. The flower has a rich rose centre shading to a paler pink with heavy flecks of crimson. The star-shaped bloom can attain 23cm/9in in diameter.

Planting depth: 45cm–1m/1¹/₂–3ft

Spread: 1.5m/5ft

Care: Provide fertile soil, full sun and avoid water splash. Divide congested plants. Generally water lilies are trouble-free but remove water lily beetles, aphids and plants affected with crown rot.

○ ❅❅❅

Nymphaea 'Rosanna Supreme': Water lily

The small star-shaped blooms have a dark dusky pink centre, lightening out towards the tips, with the outer petals light pink shading out almost to white. With its glowing yellow centre, this is an ideal selection for the garden pool. The flower is 10cm/4in in diameter and the new leaves are round and have a pleasing mottled appearance, fading out to a uniform green with age.

Planting depth: 60–75cm/2–2¹/₂ft

Spread: 1.2m/4ft

Care: Provide fertile soil, full sun and avoid water splash. Divide congested plants. Generally water lilies are trouble-free but remove water lily beetles, aphids and plants affected with crown rot.

○ ❄❄❄

Nymphaea 'Rose Arey': Water lily

The petals of this 18cm/7in stellate flower are an intense pink colour with a golden yellow centre. The leaves emerge as burgundy but eventually mature to a pleasant green. The sinus is open and the leaves attain 23cm/9in in diameter. A prolific lily if allowed to colonize and a wise selection for the medium to large pool where it may produce viable seed.

Planting depth: 60cm/2ft

Spread: 1.2m/4ft

2m/6ft
2m/6ft

Care: Provide fertile soil, full sun and avoid water splash. Divide congested plants. Generally water lilies are trouble-free but remove water lily beetles, aphids and plants affected with crown rot.

○ ❄❄❄

Nymphaea 'Rose Magnolia': Water lily

This is a selection for the large pool. The new mahogany leaf changes with maturity to a uniform green upper surface and grows up to 25cm/10in in diameter. As with many of the tuberous rhizome lilies, acceptable ratios of the pale pink flowers are only forthcoming with maturity. The flower is 10cm/4in in diameter and is cup-shaped.

Planting depth: 75cm/2½ft

Spread: 2m/6ft

Care: Provide fertile soil, full sun and avoid water splash. Divide congested plants. Generally water lilies are trouble-free but remove water lily beetles, aphids and plants affected with crown rot.

◐ ✳✳✳

Nymphaea 'Rosy Morn': Water lily

The very freely produced stellate bloom of this lily has deep dusky pink inner petals, blushing out to a pale pink on the outer petals and a golden yellow centre. The effect makes for a striking flower of up to 15cm/6in in diameter, held over a mature leaf of uniform green, with new leaves having a burgundy coloration. The leaf size is 23cm/9in, with an open sinus. It is suitable for medium-sized pools.

Planting depth: 60cm/2ft

Spread: 1m/3ft

Care: Provide fertile soil, full sun and avoid water splash. Divide congested plants. Generally water lilies are trouble-free but remove water lily beetles, aphids and plants affected with crown rot.

| ○ | ❄❄❄ |

Nymphaea **'Sirius'**: Water lily

A distinctive characteristic of this cultivar is the orange/red/maroon blotching on the upper side of the deep green leaf which is 25cm/10in in diameter. The 15cm/6in flowers which are distinctly star-shaped are a pinkish red towards the centre, becoming freckled pink on the outer petals with prominent white tips. It is a suitable variety for medium-size pools.

Planting depth: Up to 75cm/2¹⁄₂ft

Spread: Up to 2m/6ft

Care: Provide fertile soil, full sun and avoid water splash. Divide congested plants. Generally water lilies are trouble-free but remove water lily beetles, aphids and plants affected with crown rot.

○ ❄❄❄

Nymphaea 'Splendida': Water lily

The 23cm/9in diameter leaf is green with a mahogany background coloration, and a lighter mahogany underside. From the red/orange centre, the deep pink inner petals become a lighter shade of pink towards the outside, fading almost to white at the outside tips. The bloom is 15cm/6in diameter and is pleasantly fragranced.

Planting depth: 75cm/2¹/₂ft

Spread: 1.5m/5ft

Care: Provide fertile soil, full sun and avoid water splash. Divide congested plants. Generally water lilies are trouble-free but remove water lily beetles, aphids and plants affected with crown rot.

2m/6ft

2m/6ft

◗ | ❊❊❊

Nymphaea 'Sultan': Water lily

The new leaves appear bronze-green, changing to uniform green with an overlapping sinus, and are up to 30cm/12in in diameter. This prolific flowering lily has large cherry red blooms which shade to deep red at the base, with outer petals which show white towards the tips. The flower is 18cm/7in in diameter. It is a highly recommended variety for medium-sized pools.

Planting depth: Up to 75cm/2¹⁄₂ft

Spread: 1.5m/5ft

Care: Provide fertile soil, full sun and avoid water splash. Divide congested plants. Generally water lilies are trouble-free but remove water lily beetles, aphids and plants affected with crown rot.

○ ❈❈❈

With its impressive 23cm/9in diameter bloom held well above the surface of the water, this free-flowering, strong yellow water lily is ideally suited to medium or large pools. The foliage is rounded, 20cm/8in in diameter and, in common with many yellows, the green leaf often shows a burgundy speckling. The new flowers are pleasantly scented.

Planting depth: Up to 75cm/2¹/₂ft

Spread: 1.5m/5ft

Care: Provide fertile soil, full sun and avoid water splash. Divide congested plants. Generally water lilies are trouble-free but remove water lily beetles, aphids and plants affected with crown rot.

○ ❋❋❋

The stellate, 12.5cm/5in diameter, soft rose-pink bloom with its slim, lance-shaped petals and its golden centre is well set off by the spread of prolific, mid-green, distinctly veined leaves with a light mahogany shading to the undersides. The high ratio of these 15cm/6in diameter leaves to the number of flowers makes this a good selection where the amount of shade cast by foliage is an important consideration in a pool of medium size.

Planting depth: Up to 60cm/2ft

Spread: 1.2m/4ft

Care: Provide fertile soil, full sun and avoid water splash. Divide congested plants. Generally water lilies are trouble-free but remove water lily beetles, aphids and plants affected with crown rot.

78

Nymphaea **'Vivid Rose'**: Water lily

Planting this Odorata-type rhizome and allowing it to form an expanding colony encourages the production of increasing numbers of the attractive deep pink, cup-shaped, 12.5cm/5in diameter blooms. The leaf is green on the upper surface and shaded light brown on the underside. The leaf is 20cm/8in across and the sinus forms an open 'V'.

Planting depth: 60cm/2ft

Spread: 1.5m/5ft

Care: Provide fertile soil, full sun and avoid water splash. Divide congested plants. Generally water lilies are trouble-free but remove water lily beetles, aphids and plants affected with crown rot.

2m/6ft

2m/6ft

◐ ❄❄❄

With its large pale green leaf which occasionally shows small blotches on the upper surface and grows up to 30cm/12in in diameter, this is a truly big lily. Huge white blooms with a clear yellow centre are prolifically produced and attain 25cm/10in across. It also has an extra attraction in being slightly fragrant. This lily belongs in a large pond.

Planting depth: 1m/3ft

Spread: 2m/6ft

Care: Provide fertile soil, full sun and avoid water splash. Divide congested plants. Generally water lilies are trouble-free but remove water lily beetles, aphids and plants affected with crown rot.

◖ | ❊❊❊

Nymphaea 'William Falconer': Water lily

The 10cm/4in cup-shaped bloom with its burnt orange stamens and dark red petals is striking. Mature 18cm/7in leaves are a uniform green, sometimes exhibiting purple blotches which are much more prominent on the dark purple leaves when they first emerge. Generally restrained in growth, this plant is more suited to small/medium pools where it is highly prized.

Planting depth: 60cm/2ft

Spread: 1m/3ft

Care: Provide fertile soil, full sun and avoid water splash. Divide congested plants. Generally water lilies are trouble-free but remove water lily beetles, aphids and plants affected with crown rot.

○ | ❋❋❋

Nymphaea 'Yellow Princess': Water lily

With a subtle fragrance, this lily has a flower with a butter-yellow centre fading out to a light yellow. The bloom is 15cm/6in across and held over the green blotched foliage typical of yellow flowering varieties. The huge 30cm/12in diameter leaf, with its underside blotched maroon, has an open sinus. The stellate flower is held above the surface.

Planting depth: Up to 75cm/2¹/₂ft

Spread: 1.5m/5ft

Care: Provide fertile soil, full sun and avoid water splash. Divide congested plants. Generally water lilies are trouble-free but remove water lily beetles, aphids and plants affected with crown rot.

○ | ✳✳✳

Nymphaea **'Yellow Queen'**: Water lily

A number of yellow flowering water lilies exhibit attractive mottling to the upper surface of the leaf, but few can rival the degree of mottling borne on the large leaf of this variety which is 30cm/12in in diameter. The flower is equally spectacular being a very attractive yellow with a golden cupped centre, and blooms of 23–25cm/9–10in are not unusual. This prolific bloomer will open during low light levels or very early in the day.

Planting depth: 75cm/2¹/₂ft

Spread: 1.5m/5ft

Care: Provide fertile soil, full sun and avoid water splash. Divide congested plants. Generally water lilies are trouble-free but remove water lily beetles, aphids and plants affected with crown rot.

2m/6ft

2m/6ft

○ | ✳✳✳

The glaucous or blue-green, lance-shaped foliage is erect and has the ability to shed water, rolling it off in droplets. The fleshy rootstock of this aquatic produces upright rounded stems turning ebony with maturity. The distinctive flower is an erect white poker with strong golden yellow tips. It is very tolerant of a wide range of water depths. Slow to flower from seed, this plant is clump-forming. It blooms during early to mid summer.

Height × spread: 30 × 60cm/1 × 2ft or more

Position: Tolerant of differing depths of water from wet soil up to 45cm/1¹/₂ft of water, so long as it is in sun.

Care: Plant in the pool mud/water or in a basket there. Dead head the flower-spikes. Propagate by fresh seed or division.

○ ❋❋❋

Pistia stratiotes: Water lettuce

With its light green, open, lettuce-like leaf, heavily ribbed
on the surface, this tender floating plant of tropical nature
is susceptible to wind scorch and is only suitable for
summer introduction in areas which are frost-prone. Here,
the gardener must treat this decorative foliage plant as an
annual. During the summer growth can be exceptional – it
is invasive in the wild. It flowers all summer, though the
insignificant flowers are tiny.

Height × spread: 23cm/9in × indefinite spread

Position: Floating in sun in the garden pool (or in a conservatory
pool).

Care: Introduce after risk of frost and discard in winter. It requires a
minimum temperature of 10°C/50°F to thrive.

○ ❄

2.
MARGINAL PLANTS

Acorus calamus: Sweet flag

The sword-like, erect, iris-like foliage is sweetly aromatic when crushed. The flowerhead is in the form of a spadix and is insignificant. It has a creeping rhizomatous root system. The variegated form is shorter and slower growing but impressive with its green/white band variegation. It is an attractive foliage plant.

Height × spread: 1m × 60cm/3 × 2ft

Position: Up to 10cm/4in depth of water. Best in full sun.

Planting: Plant directly into the soil at the margin of the pool or stream or in a planting basket placed on a marginal shelf.

Care: Propagate by division. Clear dying foliage in autumn and divide congested plants in spring.

| ⃝ | ❊❊❊ |

Caltha palustris: Marsh marigold

This deciduous perennial produces bold tufts of dark green, kidney-shaped, toothed foliage and stout stems bearing a brilliant profusion of golden yellow-cup shaped flowers in early spring. Occasionally the plant produces a second crop of flowers. It is clump-forming in habit and one of the earliest flowering marginals in spring.

Height × spread: 30 × 30cm/1 × 1ft

Position: From wet mud to 10cm/4in of water over the crown of the plant. Best in full sun.

Planting: Plant directly into the soil at the margin of the pool or stream or in a planting basket placed on a marginal shelf.

Care: Fully hardy. Subject to mildew in summer which, whilst unsightly, has no detrimental effect, but remove old foliage to improve appearance. Propagate by seed or division.

◖ | ❋❋❋

A mound of dark green, kidney shaped and toothed foliage covered with compact, double, golden yellow blooms from early spring. Its neat and compact form and long flowering period makes this deciduous perennial essential for every pool side. Frequently this plant shows a second flush of bloom in late summer.

Height × spread: 30 × 30cm/1 × 1ft

Position: From wet mud to 10cm/4in depth of water over the crown of the plant. Best in full sun.

Planting: Plant directly into the soil at the margin of the pool or stream or in a planting basket placed on a marginal shelf.

Care: Generally trouble-free and less prone to mildew, but it is prudent to remove old foliage. Propagate by division.

○ ❋❋❋

A perennial with golden yellow, slim, grass-like leaves with a dense clump-forming habit. This cultivar produces a striking display of arching foliage which is gold with narrow green margins. The 'flower' or seed head is a brown spikelet borne on graceful tall stems. Particularly suitable for a bold architectural effect throughout the season.

Height × spread: 60 × 45cm/2 × 1½ft

Position: Poolside to 2.5cm/1in depth of water over the crown in full sun to semi-shade.

Planting: Plant directly into the soil at the margin of the pool or stream or in a planting basket placed on a marginal shelf.

Care: Remove spent foliage at the end of the year. Propagate by division in spring.

○ ◑ | E | ❄❄❄

Carex pendula: Weeping sedge

A perennial with, tall, broad, strap-like, mid-green leaves. Arching stems up to 1m/3ft long bear long, cylindrical, brown, pendulous catkin-like spikes up to 15cm/6in long. It forms large strong clumps of evergreen graceful foliage. This plant is extremely vigorous and will attain considerable stature at the poolside.

Height × spread: 1.5 × 1.5m/5 × 5ft

Position: Moist situation at the poolside in sun or part shade.

Planting: Plant directly into the soil at the margin of the pool or stream.

Care: Requires division on a regular basis to maintain best appearance. Self seeds prolifically. Propagate by division or seed. Fully hardy.

◐ ◑ | E | ❋❋❋

Carex riparia

The fresh green grass-like tall stems and dark brown seed heads makes this sedge suitable for a strong background planting. Vigorous runners create rapidly expanding clumps much favoured by dragonfly and damselfly when grown in shallow water. These strong sedges stabilize loose soil on the water edge. It is a perennial evergreen foliage plant.

Height × spread: 1 × 1m/3 × 3ft

Position: Up to 10cm/4in depth of water. Best in full sun.

Planting: Plant directly into the soil at the margin of the pool or stream but be aware of its tendency to spread.

Care: Tidy up at the end of the year. Divide congested plants in spring. Propagate by division.

◑ E ❄❄❄

This deciduous perennial with fresh green, low growing, heavily divided foliage produces masses of golden buttons all through from early to late summer. The seed quickly germinates and in combination with roots developing from the stems, the plant can rapidly expand and colonize large areas. It requires protection from frost in cold areas but self seeds to provide continuity. Excellent underplanting on wet soil.

Height × spread: 15cm/6in × indefinite spread

Position: Frost-free position in the margins of a pool. Best in full sun.

Planting: Plant directly into the soil at the margin of the pool or stream but be aware of its tendency to spread.

Care: Propagate by seed or division.

Cyperus involucratus: Umbrella grass

A tender perennial grass with a clump-forming habit and lush, rushy, fresh green, vigorous, arching leaves. The flowers are composed of a fascinating terminal whorl of arching bracts of diamond-shaped individual spikelets produced in the late summer, the seeds turning dark brown in autumn. The brown autumn foliage stands well into winter for decorative effect. Frost tender.

Height × **spread:** Up to 60 × 60cm/2 × 2ft

Position: Moist soil essential.

Planting: Plant directly into the soil at the margin of the pool or stream after frosts are over.

Care: Generally trouble-free. Propagation by division in the autumn or seed. If over-wintering, bring into the conservatory in cold regions.

Cyperus longus: Sweet galingale

This hardy evergreen has pendulous grass-like foliage with a lightly serrated edge and a pronounced mid-rib. Flower stems are triangular and convex in shape, stiffly upright, bearing grass-like spikelets which turn reddish-brown in autumn. The tall and attractive foliage which stands long into the autumn makes this one of the most handsome architectural marginals.

Height × spread: 1.2m/4ft × indefinite spread

Position: From moist soil to 20cm/8in depth of water over the crown.

Planting: Plant directly into the soil at the margin of the pool or stream but be aware of its tendency to spread.

Care: Invasive and will freely colonize large areas. Propagation is simple by division or seed.

○ ◑ | E | ❄❄❄

Equisetum scirpoides: Small horsetail

This compact, clump-forming, pool-side plant comprises a mass of dark green leaflets defined by a distinctive banding of black at each stem segment. This small evergreen perennial is the perfect foil for many low-growing flowering pool plants, providing it is contained, because of its long season and unusual foliage effect.

Height × **spread:** 30 × 23cm/1ft × 9in

Position: Wet soil to 5cm/2in depth of water.

Planting: Best planted in a basket placed on a marginal shelf so that its spread will be contained.

Care: Propagation by division.

◐ ◑ | E | ❋❋❋

Eriophorum angustifolium: Cotton grass

Cotton grass produces tough upright stems of stiff evergreen grass or rush-like leaves in loose clumps, developing in summer spikelets of cotton wool-like tufts held above the foliage. It is strongly spreading by means of the tough rhizome. An excellent accompaniment for strong rooting, broad leaf plants that can stand the competition.

Height × spread: 30cm/1ft × indefinite spread

Position: Full sun. Plant in water margins to a depth of 4in of water above the crown of the plant.

Planting: Plant directly into the soil at the margin of the pool or stream but be aware of its tendency to spread.

Care: Propagation by division in spring.

◑ E ❋❋❋

Ascending spires of dark green with a segmented stem bearing whorls of soft leathery leaves giving an almost Christmas tree-like appearance on emergent growth. Submerged leaves are very lax, vigorous in growth and will rapidly establish a small forest-like colony. Grown for its unusual form, it requires control to restrain its spread.

Height × **spread:** 60cm/2ft × indefinite spread

Position: Wet soil to 5cm/2in depth of water.

Planting: Plant in the margins of a pool but its spread must be contained.

Care: Propagate by division. Control its rapid spread as necessary.

◐ ● ❋❋❋

Houttuynia cordata 'Chameleon'

An amazing and handsome, low-growing, but loosely upright, ground cover marginal whose leaves are vividly blotched with many shades of cream, green, yellow and pink which uniformly take on a reddish tinge in autumn. The leaves are heart shaped and give off a strong scent of orange peel when bruised. The flower is white but insignificant.

Height × spread: 25cm/10in × indefinite spread

Position: Will naturalize in the pool margin and benefits from full sun, though it will tolerate part shade.

Planting: Plant directly into the soil at the margin of the pool or stream but be aware of its tendency to spread.

Care: Normally trouble-free but control its spread by removing the creeping roots. Propagation is easy by root cutting.

○ ◑   ❋❋❋

The expanding rhizome produces a slender mid-green iris leaf with a distinctive mid-rib followed by a number of deep purple or pink/purple blooms with a distinctive yellow blaze on the fall. Seed raised plants often bloom in shades of pink, purple, lavender, blue and white. The flowers, held on tall stems well above the foliage, are impressive.

Height × spread: 75 × 45cm/2$^1/_2$ × 1$^1/_2$ft

Position: Full sun or partial shade. Moist in summer; drier in winter.

Planting: Plant in soil at the margins of the water, but it needs a drier position in winter.

Care: Requires adequate moisture in the summer but will suffer in a wet situation during winter months. Division is the only reliable method of propagation to maintain the original colour.

◐◑ ❄❄❄

Iris 'Gerald Darby'

A fine, robust, water-loving cultivar with several bluish-violet flowers streaked and whiskered with white and gold, on each stem. These stems are purplish-red. The foliage is sturdy, flat and arches over. It blooms in early summer to summer. It belongs to the Laevigatae group (water iris) which enjoys moist or wet conditions. It looks at its best in a small group for a natural effect.

Height × spread: 75 × 60cm/2¹/₂ × 2ft

Position: For full sun or part shade. Grow in moist soil or shallow water, up to 10cm/4in deep.

Planting: Plant directly into the soil at the margin of the pool or in a planting basket placed on a marginal shelf.

Care: Remove dead flower stems and leaves at the end of the season. Propagate by division of the rhizomes.

○ ◑ | ✿✿✿

Iris 'Holden Clough'

A moisture-loving iris producing a heavily veined rust over its yellow bloom and typical iris foliage, semi-evergreen in a pale green shade with a discernible rib. Flowering in late spring to early summer, it is a subtle and unique addition to the iris family. Not as vigorous in growth as many of the moisture loving iris, but its almost orchid-like bloom makes it very desirable.

Height × spread: 45–75cm × 60cm/1½–2½ × 2ft

Position: Full sun to half shade in a damp poolside situation.

Planting: Plant directly into the damp soil at the margin of the pool or stream.

Care: Do not disturb unnecessarily. Slow to moderate growth. Propagation by division.

○ ◑ | Semi-E | ❄❄❄

Iris pseudacorus: Yellow flag

This strong growing iris develops tall, broad leaves with a pronounced mid-rib and robust upright stems which produce rich golden blooms in early to midsummer. It has a strong clump-forming habit and increases with maturity but sometimes at the expense of the quantity of bloom produced. Suitable for larger pools and natural plantings.

Height × spread: 1.5m × 30cm/5 × 1ft but rhizomes can spread indefinitely.

Position: From damp soil to 20cm/8in of water over the crown.

Planting: Plant directly into the soil at the margin of the pool or stream but be aware of its tendency to spread/self-sow invasively.

Care: Reliably hardy, most floriferous from young seed-raised plants. Propagation by seed or by division of the rhizomes.

◐ ❄❄❄

Iris pseudacorus 'Variegata': Variegated yellow flag

A large iris producing strap-like leaves with spectacular yellow green variegation from very early spring. Most strongly pronounced in new growth, the variegation becomes less obvious during late summer, but the contribution of this splendid plant is enhanced by the glorious golden yellow blooms in early to midsummer.

Height × spread: 1.5m × 30cm/5 × 1ft

Position: Full sun or semi-shade. From moist soil to 10cm/4in depth of water over the crown.

Planting: Plant directly into the soil at the margin of the pool or stream or in a planting basket placed on a marginal shelf.

Care: Reliably robust. Propagation by division of the rhizomes.

○ ◐ | ❄❄❄

Iris versicolor

The erect iris-like leaf is produced from a woody rhizome, the base of the foliage showing a distinctive reddish-purple colouration. Later a tall flowering branched stem is produced supporting a number of rich blue/mauve freckled flowers with a white throat and yellow blaze in early to midsummer. It is spectacular in large drifts.

Height × spread: 60 × 30cm/2 × 1ft. Flowers to 1m/3ft tall.

Position: Full sun to half shade. Grow in moist soil or shallow water.

Planting: Plant directly into the soil at the margin of the pool or stream or in a planting basket placed on a marginal shelf.

Care: To avoid rot problems remove dead foliage and woody flower stems at the end of the season. As growth radiates from a central point division on a regular basis will reduce hollow appearance. Propagation by seed or division of the rhizomes.

◯ ◑ ❄ ❄ ❄

Iris versicolor 'Kermesina'

The erect iris leaf of this perennial is produced from a woody rhizome. A reddish-purple colouration appears at the base of the leaf which has no discernible mid-rib. In early to midsummer this iris produces a tall flower stem with clusters of three to five flowers, each 7.5cm/3in across in rich purple/claret veined with white.

Height × **spread:** 60 × 30cm/2 × 1ft. Flower stems to 75cm/2¹/₂ft.

Position: Suitable for small ponds. Grow in moist soil or up to 10cm/4in depth of water above the crown.

Planting: Plant directly into the soil at the margin of the pool or stream or in a planting basket placed on a marginal shelf.

Care: Generally trouble-free, it slowly forms a clump which can become hollow in the centre and requires periodic division. Propagation by division.

◐ ◑ | ❋ ❋ ❋

Jussiaea (syn. *Ludwigia*) *grandiflora*

A perennial with a sprawling habit which has heavily veined lance-shaped leaves and produces an abundance of canary yellow blooms with five/six petals in late summer to autumn. This plant will colonize open areas of water by means of runners which will produce additional roots at intervals allowing plantlets to develop wherever permitted.

Height × spread: 23cm/9in × indefinite spread

Position: Wet soil or up to 10cm/4in depth of water.

Planting: Best planted in a basket placed on a marginal shelf so that its spread will be contained.

Care: Generally speaking this plant is trouble-free. Propagate either by cuttings or by division.

◐ ❋❋❋

Lobelia cardinalis: Cardinal flower

From basal rosettes grow strong stems in a uniform rich burgundy producing a slender, pointed and arching, burgundy leaf with a pendulous tip. The striking dark red foliage effect is even more spectacular with the profusion of scarlet flowers during mid to late summer. An excellent contrast planting for many moisture situations. Frost hardy.

Height × spread: 1m × 30cm/3 × 1ft

Position: Moist situation in semi-shade during the growing period.

Planting: Place in a planting basket so the plant can be moved in winter to a drier location.

Care: Protect from frosts and slugs. Grow in a sheltered position and stake the plants if necessary. Propagate by division or seed.

○ ◐ ❋❋

Lobelia 'Dark Crusader'

This frost-hardy perennial bears narrow, lance-shaped maroon leaves with red-bronze undersides on strong, upright, rich maroon stems in clumps. Dark red tubular flowers appear in dense racemes from mid to late summer. Associates well with hostas and ornamental clump forming grasses.

Height × spread: 1m × 30cm/3 × 1ft

Position: Sun to semi-shade in moist soil.

Planting: Place in a planting basket so the plant can be moved in winter to a drier location.

Care: Benefits from removal to a drier location during the winter period and in colder areas it requires frost protection. Take precautions against slug damage on newly emerging growth in spring. Propagate by division.

○ ◑ | ❄❄

Lobelia 'Queen Victoria'

From basal rosettes strong stems emerge in a uniform rich burgundy producing slender, pointed and arching, burgundy leaves with a pendulous tip. This striking dark red foliage is made even more spectacular by the profusion of vivid scarlet flowers during mid to late summer. An excellent contrast planting for many moisture situations. Frost hardy.

Height × spread: 1m × 30cm/3 × 1ft

Position: Moist situation in semi-shade during the growing period.

Planting: Place in a planting basket so the plant can be moved in winter to a drier location.

Care: Protect from frosts during the dormant period and from slugs during early spring. Grow in a sheltered position and stake the plants if necessary. Propagate by seed or division.

Lobelia 'Russian Princess'

This frost-hardy perennial has tall upright stems bearing slightly pendulous, lance-shaped, dark green leaves with a burgundy shading on the upper surface and distinctly burgundy undersides. The shading of the upper surface of the leaves is more pronounced on the more mature lower leaves. A profusion of large cerise to dark pink flowers appears from mid to late summer.

Height × spread: 1m × 30cm/3 × 1ft

Position: Pool-side or shallow water during the summer months, in sun or semi-shade.

Planting: Place in a planting basket so the plant can be moved in winter.

Care: Remove to a frost protected and drier location for the winter months and protect from slug damage on emerging shoots. Propagate by division.

○ ◑ ❋❋

Lobelia sessilifolia

The rigidly upright stems of this lobelia bear alternate mid-green, lance-shaped leaves with a glorious blue-purple flower produced from leaf axils right to the tip of the stem during the summer. Probably the most tolerant of all the lobelias to permanent submersion and also the most hardy of these spectacular flowering pool plants.

Height × spread: 75 × 30cm/2¹/₂ × 1ft

Position: Suitable for moist soil in sun or semi-shade or in water up to a depth of 5cm/2in.

Planting: Plant directly into the soil at the margin of the pool or stream or in a planting basket placed on a marginal shelf.

Care: It is winter hardy so does not need special winter protection. Propagate by division.

◐◑ ❅❅❅

Lobelia siphilitica: Blue cardinal flower

This clump forming perennial forms basal rosettes with erect stems bearing broad, lance-shaped, light green leaves. The narrow spires of light blue flowers are borne in strong racemes from late summer to early autumn. It is a hardy lobelia and makes an attractive contrast when planted with *Iris* and *Caltha* varieties.

Height × spread: 1m × 30cm/3 × 1ft

Position: Suitable for moist soil during the growing period in sun or semi-shade.

Planting: Plant directly into the soil or in a basket, to allow for removal to a drier place for winter.

Care: It is hardy but protect from an excess of winter wet. Propagate by division.

○ ◑ ❋❋❋

Lobelia siphilitica 'Alba'

The light green foliage with its spire-like growth produces abundant white blooms from the leaf axils. Established plants form a rosette of new growth in the early spring, each developing an upright flowering stem. Pinching out tips will encourage more abundant stem growth. The flowers make a pleasing appearance from mid to late summer.

Height × spread: 1m × 30cm/3 × 1ft

Position: Suitable for moist soil during the growing period in sun or semi-shade.

Planting: Plant directly into the soil or in a basket, to allow for removal to a drier spot for winter.

Care: It is hardy but protect from an excess of winter wet. In the early part of the year be aware of snail damage. Propagate by division.

◐ ❂❂❂

Lysichiton americanus: Yellow skunk cabbage

From a slowly enlarging clump this plant produces a spear shaped, blotched, light and mid-green leaf which is waxy on the underside when new and becomes large and fleshy as it matures. The spathes in early spring are arum-like in an attractive pale to golden yellow. It is slow to mature when produced from seed but produces many plantlets around the base of full-grown specimens.

Height × spread: 1.2 × 1.2m/4 × 4ft

Position: Suitable for moist soil in sun or semi-shade or in water up to a depth of 5cm/2in.

Planting: Plant directly into the soil at the margin of the pool or stream or in a planting basket placed on a marginal shelf.

Care: Generally trouble-free. Propagation by seed is slow but offsets can be replanted in the spring.

○ ◐ ❄❄❄

With its huge spathe in white with pale green spadix and its large, broad, ribbed, glossy, spear-shaped, leathery leaf, this impressive waterside or marginal plant associates well with *Caltha* and *Primula* species as a specimen plant. It produces a large anchorage root, is slow to establish and resents disturbance. Spathes appear in early spring.

Height × spread: 1 × 1m/3 × 3ft

Position: Suitable for moist soil in sun or semi-shade or in water up to a depth of 5cm/2in.

Planting: Plant directly into the soil at the margin of the pool or stream or in a planting basket placed on a marginal shelf.

Care: Generally trouble-free. Propagation by seed is slow but offsets can be replanted in the spring.

◐◑ ❋❋❋

This is a prostrate, evergreen, ground-cover plant with a creeping habit producing roots at nodes at intervals. The rounded leaf is bright green and the flower is cup shaped and rich yellow. It can be invasive and is shade tolerant. There is a golden leafed form, *L. n.* 'Aurea', which is slightly less vigorous and highly recommended for its leaf colour.

Height × **spread:** 7.5cm/3in × indefinite spread

Position: Suitable for moist soil in sun or semi-shade.

Planting: Plant directly into the soil at the margin of the pool or stream but be aware of its tendency to spread.

Care: Generally trouble free. Propagate by seed or division.

○ ◑ 　 ❋❋❋

This is a perennial which expands by the use of underground runners. It is a tall growing plant which produces leaves in whorls. The flowers, which are golden yellow, are produced within the leaf axils in mid to late summer. It is very vigorous and its invasive tendency needs to be controlled.

Height × **spread:** 75 × 60cm/2^1/$_2$ × 2ft

Position: Suitable for moist or wet soil. Best in full sun.

Planting: Plant directly into the soil at the margin of the pool or stream but be aware of its tendency to spread.

Care: Generally trouble-free. Propagate by seed or division.

◯ ❄❄❄

Mentha aquatica: Water mint

With its combination of low-growing, creeping stems and upright growth, this vigorous poolside plant has a distinctive mint smell and produces its profusion of tubular whorls of lilac blooms in globe-like clusters. Due to its creeping habit – it roots at intervals – this attractive plant can rapidly run riot and should be restricted.

Height × spread: 60cm/2ft × indefinite spread.

Position: Suitable for moist or wet soil or in water to a depth of 15cm/6in. Grows in full sun or part shade.

Planting: Best planted in a basket placed on a marginal shelf so that its spread will be contained.

Care: Generally trouble-free. Propagate by seed, division of rhizomes or tip cuttings.

○ ◑ | ❄❄❄

Myosotis scorpioides 'Mermaid': Water forget-me-not

This plant has a mid to dark green slightly oval hairy leaf, heavily veined with a strong mid-rib, produced on sprawling hairy stems with a reddish tinge. Flowering shoots have a tendency to form upright terminal clusters of compact, pale blue, individual blooms with a pale yellow centre. Roots are produced at any point on the stem that is in contact with the soil. Flowers throughout the summer.

Height × spread: 15–30cm/6–12in × indefinite spread

Position: Suitable for moist or wet soil or in water to a depth of 5cm/2in. Grows in full sun or part shade.

Planting: Plant directly into the soil at the margin of the pool or stream but be aware of its tendency to spread.

Care: Generally trouble-free. Propagate by division.

Myriophyllum aquaticum: Parrot's feather

Submerged stems produce many pale lax leaves from each node which towards the tip rise above the water surface and take on the rich mid-green feather-like appearance from which it gets its common name. It can put runners over considerable distances of open water, providing floating rafts for the protection of many aquatic subjects.

Height × spread: 23cm/9in × indefinite spread.

Position: Suitable for water margins to a depth of 15cm/6in or more.

Planting: Plant directly into the soil at the margin of the pool or stream but be aware of its tendency to spread.

Care: Generally trouble-free though will be invasive. Propagate by division. *M. spicatum*, also an oxygenator, is less invasive and may be preferred.

◑ ◐ | ❄❄

Phalaris arundinacea **'Picta'**: Gardener's garters

A strong growing, vigorous, spreading grass with an upright habit. The base of the stems is reddish pink whilst the stems and lance-shaped alternate leaves show distinctive parallel variegation. This perennial produces typical grass-like seed heads in summer and needs to be contained as vigorous runners are produced in profusion.

Height × **spread:** 1.5m/5ft × indefinite spread.

Position: Suitable for moist soil or water margins to a depth of 5cm/2in. Grows in full sun or part shade.

Planting: Best planted in a basket placed on a marginal shelf so that its spread will be contained.

Care: Generally trouble-free. Propagate by division.

◯ ◑ | ❋❋❋

Phragmites communis 'Variegatus'

This extremely tough reed has strong upright stems bearing golden yellow, striped green, slim, lance-shaped leaves. Spreading vigorously by numerous runners, this reed will colonize large waterside areas. Impressive plumes of silky spikelets during the latter part of the summer.

Height × spread: 1m/3ft × indefinite spread.

Position: Full sun to partial shade. Plant in water margin to a depth of 10cm/4in above the crown of the plant.

Planting: Plant directly into the soil at the margin of the pool or stream but be aware of its tendency to spread.

Care: Propagation by division only.

○ ◑ | ❋❋❋

Pontederia cordata: Pickerel weed

A broad, lance-shaped and waxy mid-green leaf is produced from a thick rhizome. This plant is recommended for its pleasing combination of architectural foliage and the profuse tubular spikes of bright blue flowers produced in summer. It is often late to appear in the early spring but continues in bloom until late season.

Height × **spread:** 1m × 75cm/3 × 2¹/₂ft

Position: Suitable for wet soil or water margins to a depth of 15cm/6in. Grows best in full sun.

Planting: Plant directly into the soil at the margin of the pool or stream or in a planting basket placed on a marginal shelf.

Care: Generally trouble-free. Propagate by division or seed.

○ | ✳✳✳

Pontederia dilatata

From a thick fleshy rhizome, strong tall stems emerge supporting narrow, lance-shaped leaves in a mid-green with evident parallel ribbing, the dense upright foliage being topped with spikes of rich blue flowers. Clump forming in habit, the glossy leaves form an excellent accent plant for the larger water garden.

Height × spread: 1.5 × 1m/5 × 3ft

Position: Suitable for wet soil or water margins to a depth of 15cm/6in. Grows best in full sun.

Planting: Plant directly into the soil at the margin of the pool or stream.

Care: Generally trouble-free. Propagate by division or seed.

◯ ❄❄❄

Preslia (syn. *Mentha*) *cervina*: Water spearmint

Sprawling stems of narrow, lance-shaped, opposite leaves and pompons of lavender flower clusters are produced in late summer. The major contribution of this plant is the distinctive scent. This is detectable most of the time, but most obvious when the plant is brushed or bruised.

Height × spread: 38cm/15in × indefinite spread.

Position: Suitable for moist soil. Grows in full sun or part shade.

Planting: Plant directly into the soil at the margin of the pool or stream but be aware of its tendency to spread.

Care: Generally trouble-free. Propagate by division in spring.

Ranunculus flammula: Lesser spearwort

This is a prolific plant with hollow semi-prostrate stems with a reddish tinge. The leaf is linear or slim lance-shaped and dark green. It produces plantlets on runners at every leaf joint with flower stems of small cup-shaped buttercup blooms in bright yellow. A vigorous and creeping deciduous perennial.

Height × spread: 60cm/2ft × indefinite spread.

Position: Suitable for wet soil or water margins to a depth of 10cm/4in. Grows in full sun or part shade.

Planting: Plant directly into the soil at the margin of the pool or stream but be aware of its tendency to spread.

Care: Generally trouble-free. Propagate by division or seed.

○ ◑ ❋❋❋

The tall flowering stems bear glossy, cup-shaped, golden yellow blooms and short-stalked, slim, lance-shaped leaves. The non-flowering stems have broader, long-stalked, oval and pointed deep green leaves. This long-flowering plant is ideal for naturalizing at the pool edge where its vigorous growth does not present a problem.

Height × **spread:** 1.2 × 2m/4 × 6ft

Position: Suitable for wet soil or water margins to a depth of 10cm/4in. Grows in full sun or part shade.

Planting: Plant directly into the soil at the margin of the pool or stream but be aware of its tendency to spread.

Care: Generally trouble-free. Propagate by division or seed.

◐◑ ❋❋❋

Sagittaria sagittifolia: Arrowhead

The distinctly shaped emergent foliage has an almost waxy, glossy green, arrowhead leaf form followed by spikes of open white simple flowers with a purple basal spot in summer. The plant produces small swollen tubers from where one of its common names of Swamp Potato is derived. It is vigorous and colonizes in shallow water where it can enlarge to impressive stands.

Height × spread: 1m/3ft × indefinite spread

Position: Suitable for water margins up to 45cm/1½ft deep.

Planting: Plant directly into the soil at the margin of the pool or stream but be aware of its tendency to spread.

Care: Generally trouble-free. Propagate by division.

○ ◑ | ❄❄❄

Saururus cernuus: Lizard tail

This plant is valuable for its flower colour in the late summer. It has drooping white pendant flower spikes over bright green heart-shaped foliage. The flowers, which resemble a slim lamb's tail, can be up to 15cm/6in long and are fragrant. When crushed the foliage is also aromatic.

Height × **spread:** 60 × 60cm/2 × 2ft

Position: Suitable for wet soil or water margins up to 5cm/2in deep.

Planting: Plant directly into the soil at the margin of the pool or stream or in a planting basket placed on a marginal shelf.

Care: Generally trouble-free. Propagate by division.

◐◑ ❄❄❄

***Scirpus lacustris* subsp. *tabernaemontani* 'Zebrinus'**: Zebra rush

From a slowly expanding clump, cylindrical upright stems with the most distinctive horizontal bands of cream against the glaucous green, justify the common name. The flower is insignificant formed of a brown grass-like burr. It is important to remove any stems failing to show this distinctive variegation as older clumps can revert to a plain green stem. Also known as *Schoenoplectus*.

Height × spread: 1m × 60cm/3 × 2ft or more

Position: Suitable for damp soil or water margins up to 5cm/2in deep.

Planting: Plant directly into the soil at the margin of the pool or stream.

Care: Generally trouble-free. Propagate by division.

○◑ ❄❄❄

Typha latifolia: Great reed mace

Ths is the familiar 'bulrush' so often seen naturalizing waterways. From the incredibly vigorous creeping rhizome columns of strap-like leaves surrounding the stem produce the familiar reed mace flower which resembles a 23cm/9in long brown poker. Flowers in late summer.

Height × spread: 2.4m/8ft × indefinite spread

Position: Suitable for water margins up to 30cm/1ft deep.

Planting: Plant directly into the soil at the margin of the pool or stream but be aware of its tendency to spread.

Care: Generally trouble-free but control its spread. Propagate by seed or division.

◐◑ ❄❄❄

Typha minima: Dwarf Japanese bulrush

While commonly called bulrush, these fine plants are reed mace. With its distinctive short cylindrical brown heads carried jauntily over upright slim stems, this plant is suitable for the smaller pool or stream-side. It expands from the creeping rootstock. The flowerhead appears during late spring or early summer.

Height × spread: 60 × 30cm/2 × 1ft or more

Position: Suitable for water margins up to 10cm/4in deep.

Planting: Plant directly into the soil at the margin of the pool or stream or in a planting basket placed on a marginal shelf.

Care: Generally trouble-free. Propagate by division.

⊙ ◑ | ❄❄❄

Veronica beccabunga: Brooklime

Brooklime has a small, slightly elongated, round leaf
produced from fleshy, creeping, burgundy-tinged stems
with a profusion of blue flowers with a white centre
produced from the leaf axils throughout the summer.
Roots forming from stems enable this pool side plant to
become a prodigious ground cover. Tends to be 'straggly'
but by relocating developing plantlets a more compact
appearance can be attained. Normally evergreen.

Height × **spread:** 25cm/10in × indefinite spread

Position: For wet soil or water margins up to 10cm/4in deep.

Planting: Plant directly into the soil at the margin of the pool or
stream but be aware of its tendency to spread.

Care: Generally trouble-free. Propagate by division.

◐ ◑ | E | ❋❋❋

Zantedeschia aethiopica 'Crowborough'

The glossy, large, arrow-shaped leaves are produced on long stems from the large rhizome and are followed in early summer by the flower in the form of a snow-white spathe with golden yellow spadix. If planted in up to 30cm/1ft of water, it can withstand most winters outdoors and in mild areas may be evergreen. If grown in damp soil, protect the crown in winter.

Height × spread: 1m × 60cm/3 × 2ft

Position: Suitable for moist soil or water margins up to 30cm/1ft deep.

Planting: Plant directly into the soil at the margin of the pool or stream or in a planting basket placed on a marginal shelf.

Care: Protect the crown in winter. Propagate by division of the rhizome.

○ ❄❄❄ (borderline)

3.
MOISTURE-LOVING PLANTS

Acanthus spinosus **Spinosissimus**: Bear's breeches

With deep green, heavily divided and prickly leaves, this clump-forming architectural plant sends up tall spikes of strong white and purple flowers to a height of 1m/3ft. These flower spikes are protected by wicked thorns. It is suitable for a full sun situation and requres adequate but not excessive moisture at the root. It flowers in summer.

Height × **spread:** 1.2m × 75cm/4 × 2¹/₂ft

Soil: Best grown in fertile, moist but well-drained soil.

Position: For moist beds and borders in sun or part-shade.

Care: Deadhead after flowering and cut down spent growth at the end of year. Propagate by seed, division or root cuttings.

◐ ◑ | ✱✱✱

From a stout, creeping rhizome the lance-shaped, mid-green fronds are produced on shiny black or very dark brown upright stalks. This vigorous fern will colonize large areas of moist soil in either a shady or open situation. It is deciduous and an ideal accompaniment to both other ferns and hosta or primula plantings. It is much favoured by flower arrangers.

Height × spread: 45 × 45cm/1¹/₂ × 1¹/₂ft

Soil: For moist but well-drained soil, enriched with humus in part shade and shelter.

Position: For moist beds and borders in part shade and shelter.

Care: Protect from heavy and prolonged frost. Propagate by division of the rhizomes in early spring if wanted.

◖ | Semi-E | LH | ❈❈/❈❈❈

***Ajuga reptans* 'Burgundy Glow'**: Bugle

This delightful ground-cover perennial forms rosettes of heavily veined and deeply ribbed spade-shaped leaves. The new growth is a rich burgundy/plum colour variegated with pink tinges. The rosettes root down where permitted with roots developing from the nodes. The bloom consists of an erect spike of small lavender blue flowers produced in spring over a long period.

Height × **spread:** 15 × 60cm/6in × 2ft

Soil: Best grown in fertile, moist but well-drained soil.

Position: For moist beds and borders near the water garden, where it can be used as an underplanting to tall plants.

Care: Deadhead after flowering. No regular pruning needed. Propagate by division.

❍◐ | Semi-E | ❄❄❄

Alchemilla mollis: Lady's mantle

This is a vigorous ground-cover perennial. With their crinkled edges, the rounded leaves form hummocks of pale green from which emerge numerous sprays of lime green/yellow flowers giving a frothy appearance in mid-summer for a long period. The small flower sprays can sometimes almost conceal the leaves beneath and are an attractive contrast to other broad-leaved plants. It will self-seed vigorously unless it is deadheaded.

Height × spread: 60 × 60cm/2 × 2ft

Soil: Best grown in fertile, moist but well-drained soil.

Position: For moist beds and borders in sun or part shade.

Care: Deadhead after flowering and cut down spent growth at the end of year. Propagate by seed, division or root cuttings.

○ ◑ ❈❈❈

Angelica archangelica

A tall stately plant, this short-lived perennial with large deeply divided leaves in mid to bright green supports a towering umbel of green/white flowers in late summer. Failure to remove flower heads before seed is set often results in the death of the plant. The stems are used when crystallized for culinary purposes. It is a splendid, tall background or feature plant. It resents disturbance.

Height × spread: 2 × 1m/6 × 3ft

Soil: Best in moist soil that is well-drained.

Position: For moist beds and borders in full sun.

Care: Deadhead after flowering. Propagate by seed. Transplant when young.

○ ❀❀❀

Arisaema candidissimum: Jack in the pulpit

From the swollen tuber an elegant, freesia-fragranced, pitcher-like, striped spathe of pink and white appears followed by broad arum-type leaves with distinctive veining. This plant is suitable for any moist soil with partial shade, but thrives if its slightly acid to neutral soil preference can be accommodated. It is only frost-hardy.

Height × spread: 45 × 15cm/1 ½ft × 6in

Soil: Best in moist soil, well-drained, enriched with humus, neutral to acid.

Position: For moist beds and borders in part shade.

Care: Mulch for protection in winter. Propagate by seed or shoots.

◐ LH ❄❄

Arum italicum: Black calla

A feature of the plant is the dark green, waxy, elongated, arrowhead leaf with pale green or cream veining which appears in the autumn and stands throughout the winter. As the flowering stalk appears the leaf will deteriorate. The spathe is greenish white with a pale yellow spadix. After fertilization numerous bright orange fruits develop and this is the only portion of the plant evident during summer.

Height × spread: 30 × 20cm/1ft × 8in

Soil: Best in moist soil that is well-drained.

Position: For moist beds and borders in sun.

Care: Mulch with humus. Propagate by seed or division after flowering.

◖ ❄❄

Aruncus dioicus: Goat's beard

This statuesque, vigorous, waterside perennial produces its palmate mid-green leaves from a woody rootstock. The flower head produced in mid to late summer is feathery and cream coloured, ageing to brown, held well above the foliage. Frequently this plant colonizes large areas by self-sown seeds.

Height × **spread:** 1.2 × 1.2m/4 × 4ft

Soil: It grows best in moist but well-drained soil.

Position: For moist beds and borders preferably in part-shade; or in sun.

Care: Deadhead after flowering and cut down spent growth at the end of year. Propagate by division.

◐ ◑ ❄❄❄

Aruncus dioicus 'Kneiffii'

This plant is very similar to *Aruncus dioicus* but has
finely cut leaves and is less robust with thin shoots and it
has smaller flowers. The large astilbe-like foliage provides
a pleasing light canopy in late spring. This plant enjoys a
part-shady position. As it is neat and compact, it is easy to
accommodate in beds and borders in the smallest garden.

Height × spread: 1m × 45cm/3 × 1¹/₂ft

Soil: It grows best in moist but well-drained soil.

Position: For moist beds and borders in part-shade, or in sun.

Care: Deadhead after flowering and cut down spent growth at the end
of year. Propagate by division.

○ ◑ ❄❄❄

Astilbe × *arendsii* 'Erica'

The glossy, dark green, lance-shaped leaves of this perennial are sharply toothed. The pink flowering panicle is formed in a loose pyramid in early and high summer and is held on stems which are tinged with red. It is a very showy waterside plant which tolerates semi-shade. Like most astilbes, it will create the maximum effect if it is planted en masse.

Height × spread: 45 × 45cm/1$\frac{1}{2}$ × 1$\frac{1}{2}$ft

Soil: It thrives in soil that is moist and rich in humus.

Position: For moist beds and borders ideally in part shade.

Care: Deadhead after flowering and cut down spent growth at the end of year. Mulch in spring. Propagate by division.

◑ | ❄❄❄

Astilbe × arendsii 'Granat'

This plant has a glossy, bronzed, broad leaf, sharply
toothed. The individual flowers are deep red and tiny but
produced on towering spikes in panicles which gives a
striking massed effect. This plant associates well with
other green-leafed astilbes for foliage effect, making a
handsome contrast. Like all astilbes, it is unlikely to thrive
in soil that is chalky.

Height × spread: 60 × 45cm/2 × 1¹/₂ft

Soil: It grows best in moist and humus-rich soil.

Position: For moist beds and borders ideally in part shade.

Care: Deadhead after flowering and cut down spent growth at the end
of year. Mulch in spring. Propagate by division.

◑ ❄❄❄

Astilbe 'Deutschland'

This fine perennial has glossy, dark green, lance-shaped leaves, sharply toothed, on stems which are tinged red. The flowering panicle forms a loose pyramid in early or high summer. A showy white waterside plant which can tolerate semi-shade. When planted en masse it will produce a dramatic effect which will be reinforced by its reflection if it is near water.

Height × spread: 45 × 30cm/1½ × 1ft

Soil: It thrives in soil that is moist and rich in humus.

Position: For moist beds and borders ideally in part shade.

Care: Deadhead after flowering and cut down spent growth at the end of year. Mulch in spring. Propagate by division.

◐ ✳✳✳

Astilbe 'Montgomery'

The mass of mid-green foliage bears flowering stems of dense feathery plumes of deep red. This is often left to stand into the winter when they retain their form but the plumes become a pleasing rust brown. It is very similar to *Astilbe japonica* except that it is taller and the plumes are a different colour.

Height × spread: 75 × 75cm/2¹/₂ × 2¹/₂ft

Soil: It grows best in moist but well-drained soil.

Position: For moist beds and borders ideally in part shade.

Care: Deadhead after flowering and cut down spent growth at the end of year. Mulch in spring. Propagate by division.

◐ ❋❋❋

Astrantia major: Masterwort

From a lower-growing clump of foliage, stiffly erect stems are produced with star-like bracts surrounding each whitish, green-tinged-with-pink flower. The leaf is heavily divided and mid-green. This perennial enjoys a sunny or part-shady location and moist soil. The flowers can be dried and used in flower arrangements.

Height × spread: 60 × 60cm/2 × 2ft

Soil: It grows best in moist but well-drained, humus-rich soil.

Position: For moist beds and borders in sun or part-shade.

Care: Deadhead after flowering and cut down spent growth at the end of year. Propagate by division.

○ ◐ ❉❉❉

Blechnum tabulare: Hard fern

The clump-forming rhizome of this frost-hardy fern
produces first upright and then spreading fronds. It has a
palm-like appearance with the lance-shaped leaves in
pairs along the frond. This plant requires adequate
moisture during the growing season but benefits from a
drier situation during the winter. An impressive graceful
effect is given by the evergreen or semi-evergreen foliage.

Height × spread: 1m × 60cm/3 × 2ft

Soil: It grows best in moist but well-drained soil, humus-rich and acidic
to neutral.

Position: For moist beds and borders in part shade or full shade.

Care: Cut down spent growth as necessary. Propagate by spores in
late summer.

◐ ● | Semi-E/E | LH | ❄❄

Cardamine pentaphyllos

The mid to dark green leaf of this perennial is palmate,
each leaflet being lance-shaped. It has loose racemes of
pale lilac or purple flowers in late spring or early summer.
This plant associates extremely well with many of the
low-growing and clump-forming decorative grasses which
are so popular for moist soil planting situations.

Height × **spread:** 45 × 45cm/1 1/2 × 1 1/2ft

Soil: It grows best in moist but well-drained soil.

Position: For moist beds and borders in part shade preferably.

Care: Deadhead after flowering and cut down spent growth.
Propagate by division after flowering.

◐ | ✳✳✳

Cimicifuga simplex: Bugbane

This clump-forming perennial has irregularly lobed leaflets in a light green on upright and arching stems with bottle brush racemes of white flowers in late summer and autumn. Due to its tall stature and loose leaf habit, this is recommended for a background planting with its towering flower spires. Both flowers and leaves are often used in flower arranging.

Height × **spread:** 1.2m × 60cm/4 × 2ft

Soil: It grows best in moist but well-drained soil.

Position: For moist beds and borders, especially in woodland, in part shade.

Care: Deadhead after flowering and cut down spent growth at the end of the year. Propagate by division in spring.

◐ ❄❄❄

Cortaderia selloana: Pampas grass

Dense clumps of long, narrow, strap-like leaves on this
perennial grass form a graceful base from which cane-like
flowering stems up to 2.4m/8ft tall carry pyramidal
plumes of silver white in late summer and autumn.
Moisture during the growing season is necessary but avoid
damp winter conditions where waterlogged clumps will
fail. Benefits from frequent division.

Height × spread: 2.4 × 1.5m/8 × 5ft

Soil: It grows best in moist but well-drained soil. Avoid winter
waterlogging.

Position: For moist beds and borders near the water garden, in full sun.

Care: Cut down spent growth and protect the plant from frost.
Propagate by seed in spring or division in autumn.

○ ❄❄

Corydalis flexuosa

The stunning, light powder-blue, tubular flowers with
attractive white throats are prolifically produced from
early spring to midsummer over light green leaflets which
show an occasional tinge of purple. The leaves are ovate
and glaucous and up to 15cm/6in long. The plant then
dies right back for a period of summer dormancy.

Height × spread: 30 × 25cm/1ft × 10in

Soil: It grows best in moist but well-drained soil, enriched with humus.

Position: For moist beds and borders in part shade.

Care: As it is dormant in summer, its position may need marking.
Propagate by division in autumn.

◑ ❄❄❄

Darmera peltata: Umbrella plant

An interesting and unusual poolside addition, this plant presents in spring a number of reddish hued stalks from a dark woody creeping root stock, which bear attractive pink star-like flowers in rounded clusters about 60cm/2ft high. After flowering, the impressive round umbrella-like leaves appear. Each leaf my be 30cm/1ft in diameter and held up to 1m/3ft or more off the ground.

Height × spread: 1.2 × 1m/4 × 3ft

Soil: It grows best in moist or boggy soil.

Position: For moist beds and borders near the water garden, in sun or part shade.

Care: Cut down spent growth at the end of year. Propagate by seed or division.

◐◑ ❋❋❋

Dicentra cucullaria: Dutchman's breeches

From a rhizome or small fleshy tubers the fern-like, grey-green, heavily divided foliage forms a small mound from which arching stems bearing small, divided, white flowers with a yellow tip are produced in spring. This plant dies back after flowering and remains dormant in summer.

Height × spread: 15 × 25cm/6 × 10in

Soil: For humus-rich soil, neutral to alkaline, and gritty.

Position: For moist beds and borders, but dry in summer. For part shade.

Care: Allow to die down and keep dry in summer: moist at other times. Propagate by seed in spring, transplanting in early autumn.

◑ ❋❋❋

Dicentra spectabilis: Bleeding heart

This popular, showy, spring-flowering perennial has attractive fern-like divided leaves in grey-green, the tuberous clump topped with graceful arching pendant stems bearing rose pink and white flowers. After flowering top growth will fade, yellow and die back completely and remain dormant throughout the summer. There is also a white cultivar called *D. spectabilis* f. *alba*.

Height × spread: 1m × 45cm/3 × 1 1/2ft

Soil: It grows best in moist soil that is rich in humus and fertile.

Position: For moist beds and borders in part shade.

Care: As the plant is dormant in summer, its position may need marking. Propagate by seed in spring, transplanting in autumn.

◑ ❋❋❋

Dierama pulcherrimum: Angel's fishing rod

From a large corm a clump of arching grass-like evergreen leaves form a graceful mound from which tall, but pendulous, stems bearing pink or pink/white or pink/purple bell-shaped flowers appear. The leaves can be up to 1m/3ft high, the flower stalks up to 1.5m/5ft tall. This plant only requires moisture in summer and prefers a well-drained soil. It resents disturbance. It is frost-hardy.

Height × **spread:** 1.5m × 60cm/5 × 2ft

Soil: It grows best in moist but well-drained soil.

Position: For moist beds and borders that are in full sun and sheltered.

Care: Deadhead after flowering and cut down dead growth in late winter/spring and mulch to protect against frost.

| ◯ | E | ❋❋ |

Resembling the primula to which it is closely related in its growth habit, this hardy perennial has kidney-shaped mid-green leaves followed by prolific, rich rose, cyclamen-like flowers with reflexed petals, produced in umbels in late spring. This low-growing clump-forming plant dies back completely in summer.

Height × **spread:** 25 × 15cm/10 × 6in

Soil: It grows best in moist but well-drained soil, enriched with humus.

Position: For moist beds and borders that are in part shade.

Care: Deadhead after flowering. Allow to dry during its period of dormancy. Propagate by seed or division.

◑ ❋❋❋

The pale to mid-green, toothed, ovate leaves which are up to 23cm/9in long are presented in compact clumps. The upright stems produce umbels of creamy white strongly reflexed blooms with dark centres. After fertilization the flowers turn upwards. Immediately after flowering in late spring the plant enters a dormant period and dies down completely.

Height × spread: 25 × 15cm/10 × 6in

Soil: It grows best in moist but well-drained soil, enriched with humus.

Position: For moist beds and borders that are in part shade.

Care: Deadhead after flowering. Allow to dry during its period of dormancy. Propagate by seed or division.

◑ ❄❄❄

Eupatorium cannabinum: Hemp agrimony

Strong upright stems bear lance-shaped leaves on a perennial with a woody rhizome. The flower is a loose, false umbel of pink to pinkish-red and is carried for a long period in summer through to the autumn. This stately plant can colonize by seeding large areas of suitably moist soil and control is advised, otherwise it may be too invasive.

Height × spread: 1.5 × 1.2m/5 × 4ft

Soil: It grows best in moist soil of any kind.

Position: For moist beds and borders near the water garden, or the wild garden, in sun or part shade.

Care: Deadhead after flowering and cut down spent growth at the end of year. Propagate by seed, division or cuttings midsummer to autumn.

◐◑ ❄❄❄

Eupatorium purpureum: Joe Pye weed

With bluish-green strong upright stems with a purple-brown coloration at the leaf joints and sometimes up the stem itself, this tall growing plant sends up loose domed flower heads in shades of pink, off white or purple pink in late summer to early autumn. The leaf is mid-green, lance-shaped with a vanilla scent when crushed. It is a bold, robust perennial.

Height × spread: 2 × 1m/6 × 3ft

Soil: It grows in moist soil which has preferably some alkalinity.

Position: For moist beds and borders near the water garden, or the wild garden, in sun or part shade.

Care: Deadhead after flowering and cut down spent growth at the end of year. Propagate by seed, division or cuttings.

○ ◑   ❋❋❋

Euphorbia griffithii 'Fireglow': Spurge

With its impressive orange-red bracts in the early summer
followed by its reddish tinge to the tapering leaves in
autumn, this hardy spreading perennial has a real part to
play in poolside planting where moist soil and light shade
are available. With its dual season of interest it is an
excellent plant. Please note that the milky sap can be an
irritant to skin and is poisonous.

Height × spread: 1 × 1m/3 × 3ft

Soil: It grows best in moist, but fertile soil, enriched with humus.

Position: For moist beds and borders that are in part shade.

Care: Cut down spent growth at the end of year. Propagate by
division or cuttings.

◐ ❄❄❄

Euphorbia sikkimensis: Spurge

This perennial produces its lance-shaped early leaves from light pink shoots and, as they become mature, these leaves develop to a lighter green with red veining forming an upright spreading plant. The small individual terminal flowers are held in clusters which are up to 7.5cm/3in across and are pale yellowish-green produced from mid to late summer, providing a long season of interest.

Height × spread: 1.2m × 45cm/4 × 1½ft

Soil: It grows best in moist soil, which has some humus content.

Position: For moist beds and borders that are in part shade ideally, though it will grow in sun.

Care: Deadhead after flowering and cut down spent growth at the end of year. Propagate by division in early spring.

◑ ❄❄❄

Fargesia (syn. *Sinarundinaria*) *nitida*: Bamboo

An evergreen bamboo which is distinguished for its slim, elegant, green leaves and mid-green canes with purple stalks, erect but arching with foliage towards their ends. It is hardy but requires shelter against cold cutting winter winds. It is not invasive though the rhizomes will spread somewhat in suitable soil and can be dug out. The old canes can be used for stakes in the garden.

Height × spread: 2.4–4 × 1.5+m/8–13 × 5+ft

Soil: For fertile soil that is moist but not waterlogged.

Position: For part shade and shelter, and looks well arching near the pool.

Care: Check any excessive spread if desired and lift sections to replant in the spring.

Filipendula rubra 'Venusta': Queen of the prairie

This beautiful perennial bears a large astilbe-like, feathery plume head up to 2m/6ft high consisting of a mass of tiny dark pink flowers. The leaf is mid-green, jagged with three to five lobes. The tall branching stems and dense clump-forming habit combine to create an impressive bog or waterside plant. It is a robust grower.

Height × spread: 2 × 1m/6 × 3ft

Soil: It grows best in moist or wet, boggy soil.

Position: For moist beds and borders near the water garden, that are in sun or part shade.

Care: Deadhead after flowering and cut down spent growth at the end of year. Propagate by division in autumn or cuttings in spring.

◐◑ ❀❀❀

Filipendula ulmaria: Meadowsweet

From a woody rhizome this perennial sends up multiple upright stems bearing heavily veined and toothed leaves in a pleasing mid-green, supporting a tall flower stem bearing the feathery beard-like white or creamy bloom. In dense corymbs these give an almost cloud-like appearance over the mound of base foliage. It blooms in summer.

Height × spread: Up to 1m × 60cm/3 × 2ft

Soil: It grows best in moist or wet, boggy soil.

Position: For moist beds and borders near the water garden. It is ideal for colonizing the banks of water features. For sun or part shade.

Care: Deadhead after flowering and cut down spent growth at the end of year. Propagate by division.

○ ◑ ❋❋❋

Fritillaria meleagris: Snake's head fritillary

From a small bulb, slim, scattered, lance-like, grey-green leaves with parallel veining appear, followed by a bell-shaped pendant flower with a prominent chequered pattern in wine and pink shades. This small attractive spring-flowering bulb appears at its best when allowed to naturalize. There is also a beautiful white form, called *F.m. alba*.

Height × spread: 30 × 5–7.5cm/1ft × 2–3in

Soil: It grows best in moist but well-drained soil.

Position: For moist beds and borders in sun or part shade, or in grass where it can naturalize.

Care: Allow to seed after flowering. Propagate by seed or bulbils.

◐ ◑ ❀❀❀

The flowers on this perennial are notable for their unique blue shading from light to dark blue and are produced in profusion from mid to late summer against a background of lance-shaped, dull green foliage. This clump-forming plant provides an attractive focal point when associated with foliage plants and those which have flowered earlier in the season.

Height × spread: Up to 1m × 45cm/3 × 1¹/₂ft

Soil: It grows best in moist but well-drained soil, with a rich humus content.

Position: For moist beds and borders in part shade.

Care: Deadhead after flowering and cut down spent growth at the end of year. Propagate by seed, division or cuttings.

◑ ✳✳✳

Gentiana sino-ornata

From a compact rosette producing a mass of slim, lance-shaped leaves of dark green, single, open trumpet blooms are produced in deep blue with heavy stripes of purple/white in the throat. This autumn-flowering semi-evergreen alpine requires neutral to semi-acid soil that remains cool and moist. There is also a white form of this plant.

Height × spread: 7.5 × 20cm/3 × 8in

Soil: It grows best in moist but well-drained soil, which is rich in humus and neutral to semi-acid.

Position: For moist beds and borders in part shade.

Care: Mulch with humus. Divide the plant every three years.

◐ | Semi-E | LH | ❄❄❄

Geranium endressii: Cranesbill

From its long creeping rhizome, the deeply cut, apple green leaf with its almost glossy appearance forms an effective weed suppressant, acting as an evergreen ground cover. Flowering shoots appear along the stems and form bright pink, cup-shaped veined flowers in early to midsummer and later. A natural colonizer of moist areas, it can require control.

Height × spread: 45 × 60cm/1 1/2 × 2ft

Soil: It grows best in moist but well-drained soil.

Position: For moist beds and borders in sun or part shade.

Care: Deadhead after flowering and cut down spent growth at the end of year. Propagate by seed, division or stem cuttings.

○ ◑ | ❄❄❄

Geranium himalayense 'Gravetye': Cranesbill

From a short rhizome, dense tufts of deeply parted leaves in a pleasing green form a mound topped by large deep blue flowers on tall stems. This clump-forming perennial is particularly suited as a foreground planting due to its low spreading nature and its long flowering season, starting in early summer and continuing on and off until autumn when the leaves also tend to colour.

Height × spread: 30 × 45–60cm/1 × 1¹/₂–2ft

Soil: It grows best in moist but well-drained soil.

Position: For moist beds and borders in sun.

Care: Deadhead after flowering and cut down spent growth at the end of year. Propagate by cuttings, or division of rhizome.

◐ ❄❄❄

This plant is more upright in habit than *Geum rivale* (see p. 176) the lower leaf being smaller than the terminal leaflets. It produces cup-shaped, red/orange flowers on slim elegant stems up to 45cm/1½ft high. While this is a true moisture plant, it will show a remarkable resistance to drought conditions. It flowers for a long period from late spring to late summer.

Height × spread: 30–45 × 30cm/1–1½ × 1ft

Soil: It grows best in moist but well-drained soil.

Position: For moist beds and borders in sun.

Care: Deadhead after flowering and cut down spent growth at the end of year. Propagate by division in autumn or spring.

◯ ❋❋❋

Geum 'Red Wings': Avens

This avens forms clumps similar to those of *Geum* 'Borisii' and bears semi-double, scarlet flowers emerging from the prominent red calyces throughout the summer. It is impressive with its light green leaf and provides a pleasing addition amongst other low-growing ground-cover plantings. It is a hybrid of *Geum coccineum*.

Height × spread: 45–60 × 45cm/1½–2 × 1½ft

Soil: It grows best in moist but well-drained soil.

Position: For moist beds and borders at the pool edge, and in sun.

Care: Deadhead after flowering and cut down spent growth at the end of year. Propagate by division.

○ ❄❄❄

Geum rivale: Water avens

With its strawberry-like leaf produced on long runners in an aquatic situation, this straggly, naturalizing plant with its red to dark pink flower emerging from the prominent red-brown calyces in spring, loves the pool edge. It is a charmer, and makes a pleasing addition amongst other low-growing, ground-cover plantings. The white form of this plant is also to be admired, with creamy flowers.

Height × spread: 45 × 45cm/1¹/₂ × 1¹/₂ft

Soil: It grows well in moist to wet soil, and also in shallow running water.

Position: For moist beds and situations in the water garden, in sun or part shade.

Care: Deadhead after flowering and cut down spent growth at the end of year. Propagate by seed or cuttings.

◐ ❋❋❋

Glaucidium palmatum

This slow-growing perennial with its toothed, palmate, light green wrinkled leaf produces solitary terminal poppy-like blooms with gold stamens and a pale lilac flower. Susceptible to wind scorch, this woodland plant requires shade (even deep shade) and must have its requirement for moist soil met. There is also a white form of this plant.

Height × spread: 45 × 45cm/1½ × 1½ft

Soil: It grows best in moist soil, that is enriched with humus.

Position: For moist, shaded beds and borders near the water garden, that are sheltered from cold winds.

Care: Mulch annually and protect from cutting winds. Propagate by seed or division.

◑ ● | ❄❄❄

Gunnera manicata

With its leaf stem of up to 2m/6ft long supporting a coarse, heavily veined leaf that can attain 1.5m/5ft across, this attractive giant foliage plant for the pool edge is deservedly popular. To attain this impressive stature, it requires protection from strong winds and adequate moisture during the growing season. The large rhizome needs protection from the wet during the winter.

Height × **spread:** 2.4 × 3m/8 × 10ft

Soil: It grows best in moist soil, that has a rich humus content.

Position: For moist beds and borders near the water garden, in sun.

Care: To protect from frost, cut down and cover the crowns with the spent growth at the end of year. Propagate by seed or division.

◑ ❋❋/❋❋❋

Hosta 'Frances Williams': Plantain lily

This hosta has a leaf of grey/green with a dark yellow wide margin. It is a fine example of this large group of waterside foliage plants, distinguished by their clump-forming habit and architectural foliage. A requirement for all of them is moist soil and often partial shade. The pale yellow discoloration after the first frost is a bonus. *H.* 'Frances Williams' which is a *H. sieboldiana* hybrid has lilac flowers in summer.

Height × spread: 75 × 75cm/2$\frac{1}{2}$ × 2$\frac{1}{2}$ft

Soil: It grows best in moist, humus-rich soil.

Position: For moist beds and borders that are in part shade.

Care: Deadhead after flowering and cut down spent growth at the end of year. Mulch in spring. Protect from slugs. Propagate by division of the clump.

◐ ❋❋❋

This hosta has a typical clump-forming habit and its leaf is a pleasing soft uniform yellow with a narrow green margin. The large, deeply parallel-veined and winged leaf is waxy in appearance and it is an ideal poolside feature plant. The flowers borne on stems up to 1m/3ft long in summer are a pale lilac, funnel-shaped. The leaves retain their coloration well.

Height × spread: 75 × 75cm/2$^{1}/_{2}$ × 2$^{1}/_{2}$ft

Soil: It grows best in moist and humus-rich soil.

Position: For moist beds and borders that are in part shade.

Care: Deadhead after flowering and cut down spent growth at the end of year. Mulch in spring. Protect from slugs. Propagate by division of the clumps.

Hosta 'Halcyon': Plantain lily

This hosta bears leaves of exceptionally good coloration and form, being gunmetal blue-green and heart-shaped. They are marked with parallel veins and there is an almost indiscernible white margin. Pale lilac flowers are produced in clusters in mid to later summer. Its alternative colouring and architectural elegance give it significance and make it a highly desirable perennial.

Height × spread: 45 × 45cm/1^1/$_2$ × 1^1/$_2$ft

Soil: For moist soil that has a good humus content.

Position: For moist beds and borders that are in part or full shade.

Care: Deadhead after flowering and cut down spent growth at the end of year. Mulch in spring. Protect from slugs. Propagate by division of the clump.

◑ ● ❄❄❄

Hosta sieboldiana: Plantain lily

The large leaves are ideal for creating a strong architectural impression at the poolside. The plant has a strong clump-forming habit, and with its heavily ribbed bluish/grey foliage and attractive pale lilac blooms in early summer it is particularly suited to a shady or semi-shady location. In full sun the leaf may lose its bluish/grey coloration and can bleach to a less attractive dull green.

Height × spread: 1 × 1m/3 × 3ft

Soil: It grows best in moist and humus-rich soil.

Position: For moist beds and borders that are in part or full shade.

Care: Deadhead after flowering and cut down spent growth at the end of year. Mulch in spring. Protect from slugs. Propagate by division of the clump.

◐ ● ❋❋❋

Hosta undulata **var.** *undulata*: Plantain lily

The young foliage of this impressive hosta appears first with white blotches in the leaf centre; later the foliage bears distinctive streaks. The light stalks have narrow green margins. The lance-shaped leaf which is deeply ribbed has a distinctive green and white variegation. The flower which appears in summer is an impressive lilac.

Height × spread: 45 × 45cm/1¹/₂ × 1¹/₂ft

Soil: It grows best in moist and humus-rich soil.

Position: For moist beds and borders that are in part or full shade.

Care: Deadhead after flowering and cut down spent growth at the end of year. Mulch in spring. Protect from slugs. Propagate by division of the clump.

◐ ● ❋❋❋

Hydrangea macrophylla **'Blue wave'**: Lacecap hydrangea

This large deciduous shrub is broadly rounded in shape and the coarsely toothed dark green leaf is an ideal backcloth for the numerous flattened corymbs of flowers up to 15cm/6in across. A wonderful contrast is provided, as sterile flowers within the corymb are a pale pink and fertile flowers are a beautiful rich blue/mauve.

Height × spread: 2 × 2m/6 × 6ft

Soil: It grows best in moist, humus-rich soil. Acid soil produces the richest blue shades.

Position: For moist beds or borders that are well-drained, in sun or part shade.

Care: Deadhead in spring and prune or remove damaged or dead growth at the same time.

○ ◑ ❄❄❄

Imperata cylindrica 'Rubra': Japanese blood grass

This clump-forming perennial grass has linear mid-green leaves. The real benefit when planted in a sunny situation is the deep red discoloration which commences at the tip of the leaves progressing towards the base. It has a typical grass-like bloom of silvery spikelets in late summer.

Height × spread: 45 × 30cm/1 1/2 × 1ft

Soil: It grows best in fertile moisture-retentive soil which does not dry out but is well-drained.

Position: For moist beds and borders that are in sun or in part shade.

Care: Cut down spent growth to ground level in the early spring. Propagate by division in spring.

○ ◑ ❋❋❋

This small iris with its dense spreading habit of near evergreen upright foliage which has an unpleasant smell when crushed, has insignificant washed-out lilac coloured blooms, but these develop to produce an opening seed head of attractive orange/red in the late summer lasting for a long period which is its main appeal. It will self-seed.

Height × **spread:** 30 × 30cm/1 × 1ft or more.

Soil: It grows best in moist but well-drained soil, though also tolerates dry conditions.

Position: For moist beds and borders that are in part shade, though full shade is tolerated.

Care: Cut down dead leaves as required. Propagate by seed or division.

◑ E ❆❆❆

Iris missouriensis

This beardless iris has typical narrow upright leaves and the flower is normally grown under their canopy. Each upright stem bears more than a single bloom, and the falls of the bloom are pale lilac to lilac/purple with deep purple veining and yellow veins in the throat. The standards are shorter and pale lilac or purple. It flowers in summer.

Height × spread: 45 × 45cm/1¹/₂ × 1¹/₂ft

Soil: It grows best in moisture-retentive soil, that is also well-drained.

Position: For moist beds and borders that are in sun.

Care: Deadhead after flowering and cut down spent growth at the end of year. Propagate by division.

○ ❄❄❄

Iris setosa

This beardless iris with its erect, linear, mid-green leaf, often showing reddish tinges at the base, produces its blooms in early summer. Each flowering stem bears numbers of typical iris blooms up to 7.5cm/3in across. The large falls are in shades of blue, or blue-purple with white speckling in the throat, and the standards are small.

Height × spread: 60 × 30cm/2 × 1ft but variable.

Soil: It grows best in moisture-retentive soil.

Position: For moist beds and borders at the waterside, that are in sun.

Care: Deadhead after flowering and cut down spent growth at the end of year. Propagate by division.

◐ ❅❅❅

Iris 'Sibirica Alba': Siberian iris

The 45cm/1½ft upright grass-like leaf of this iris has a pronounced mid-rib. The single tall flower stem with its one or two branches towards the tip produces a number of showy large white flowers up to 7.5cm/3in across. These flowers are held well above the foliage in early summer. A stately plant for the pool or stream edge.

Height × spread: 75 × 30+cm/2½ × 1+ft

Soil: It grows best in moist but well-drained soil.

Position: For moist beds and borders that are in sun or part shade.

Care: Deadhead after flowering and cut down spent growth at the end of year. Propagate by division.

○ ◑ | ✿✿✿

***Iris sibirica* 'Soft Blue'**: Siberian iris

This fine example of an incredibly extensive colour range of waterside moisture-loving irises shares all of the *I. sibirica* characteristics – a need for moist soil, but not in a submerged position, full sun to partial shade, room to expand by means of the spreading rhizome. It is best planted in groups or drifts to achieve the maximum effect. It flowers in early to midsummer.

Height × spread: 60 × 30+cm/2 × 1+ft

Soil: It grows best in moist but well-drained soil.

Position: For moist beds and borders that are in sun or part shade.

Care: Deadhead after flowering and cut down spent growth at the end of year. Propagate by division.

○◐ ❄❄❄

This multi-stemmed perennial with its leaf resembling a sycamore's has a shrub-like appearance. Its leafy stems present an upright purple branchlet from which numerous pale yellow, waxy, bell or funnel-shaped blooms appear. Whilst hardy, the leaf and flower need protection from wind chill and a moist lime-free soil. It flowers in late summer to autumn.

Height × spread: 1m × 75cm/3 × 2¹/₂ft

Soil: It grows best in moist but well-drained soil, humus-rich and lime-free.

Position: For shady moist beds and borders.

Care: Deadhead after flowering and cut down spent growth at the end of year. Propagate by seed or division.

◐ ● | LH | ✳✳✳

With its spectacular bottlebrush-like flowers of soft yellow and white, this is an upright hybrid hot poker, formed from a stout rhizome with foliage resembling a large grass-like clump. It is particularly suited to a moderately moist poolside situation. The flowers appear in late summer and early autumn.

Height × spread: 60 × 45cm/2 × 1½ft

Soil: It grows best in moist but well-drained soil.

Position: For moist beds and borders that are in sun.

Care: Deadhead after flowering and cut down spent growth at the end of year. Propagate by division.

◯ | ✳✳✳

Kniphofia triangularis (syn. *K. galpinii*): Red hot poker

This deciduous perennial forms a grass-like clump of arching linear leaves, from which the slim upright stems are prolifically produced. Dense racemes of burnt-orange-red bottlebrush clusters of tubular flowers develop which tend to fade to pale yellow at the tip. This late summer/early autumn flowering plant is fully hardy.

Height × spread: 75 × 45cm/2¹/₂ × 1¹/₂ft

Soil: It grows best in moist but well-drained soil.

Position: For moist beds and borders that are in sun.

Care: Deadhead after flowering and cut down spent growth at the end of year. Propagate by division.

◯ ❄❄❄

Lamium maculatum 'White Nancy': Dead nettle

The semi-evergreen, low-growing and ground-covering foliage of this mat-forming perennial has a silver leaf with a narrow green edge and veining. The snow white flowers are borne in clusters in late spring. This plant requires part shade and will not tolerate excessive moisture in the soil in winter.

Height × spread: 15cm × 1m/6in × 3ft

Soil: It grows best in moist but well-drained soil.

Position: For the front of shady beds and borders where it can be an underplanting for taller plants.

Care: Deadhead after flowering and cut down spent growth at the end of year. Propagate by division or cuttings.

◑ | Semi-E | ❄❄❄

Leucojum aestivum: Summer snowflake

A small bulb producing long, narrow, strap-like leaves of dark green with flowering stems bearing large, white bell-like blooms, each petal tipped with green, which resemble a very large snowdrop, in early summer. These moisture-loving bulbs are ideal for pool edges and will colonize suitably moist areas from bulbils and seed. It associates well with broad-leafed poolside plantings.

Height × spread: 45–60 × 10cm/1¹/₂–2ft × 4in

Soil: It grows best in moist, humus-rich soil.

Position: For moist beds and borders near the water garden, that are in part shade.

Care: Deadhead after flowering and cut down spent growth at the end of year. Propagate by seed or division.

◑ | ❋❋❋

Leucojum vernum: Spring snowflake

This bulbous perennial has early leaves, daffodil-like, narrow and linear, of a glossy dark green. They are produced in early spring with generally solitary flower-bearing stems, with a large white bell flower with the petal having a delightful green tip. The flower can be up to 2.5cm/1in and is suspended in the manner of a pendant, resembling a snowdrop.

Height × spread: 20 × 7.5cm/8 × 3in

Soil: It grows best in moist, humus-rich soil.

Position: For moist beds and borders that are in part shade.

Care: Deadhead after flowering and cut down spent growth at the end of year. Propagate by division in spring or early autumn.

◑ ❊❊❊

Liatris spicata 'Kobold': Gayfeather

With its strong upright stems densely clothed in narrow grass-like leaves and its bottlebrush spikes of violet flowers, this spectacular moisture-lover gives a superb late summer to early autumn blaze of colour for the pool edge. Many other cultivars are available with white, purple or violet flowers which can grow up to 1.5m/5ft high and are suitable for the large garden.

Height × spread: 45 × 45cm/1$\frac{1}{2}$ × 1$\frac{1}{2}$ft

Soil: It grows best in moist but well-drained soil.

Position: For moist beds and borders that are in sun.

Care: Deadhead after flowering and cut down spent growth at the end of year.

○ ❄❄❄

Ligularia dentata 'Desdemona'

The large heart-shaped leaf of this perennial is distinctive for its dark green upper surface with a rich purple underside, borne on tall purple stems. The flower is large and daisy-like, of a deep orange/yellow, held on branched stems. This clump-forming plant can attain 1m/3ft and is fully hardy. Flowering in late summer, it can be used to impressive and showy effect.

Height × spread: 1 × 1m/3 × 3ft

Soil: It grows best in moist but well-drained soil.

Position: For moist beds and borders that are in sun or in part shade.

Care: Deadhead after flowering and cut down spent growth at the end of year. Propagate by division.

○ ◑ ❋❋❋

Ligularia stenocephala 'The Rocket'

This important waterside foliage and flowering plant has dark, almost black, flowering stems with tall spires of golden yellow flowers over a large rounded leaf cut around its edges. It is robust and with its impressive stature, it associates well with many of the larger grasses. It flowers in mid to late summer.

Height × spread: 1.5 × 1m/5 × 3ft

Soil: It grows best in moist and fertile soil.

Position: For moist beds and borders that are in sun or in part shade.

Care: Deadhead after flowering and cut down spent growth at the end of year. Propagate by division.

○ ◑ ❄❄❄

Limnanthes douglasii: Poached egg flower

To include a self-seeding annual in a collection of water plants could appear misguided. However, our own experience with the phenomenal growth of this attractive low-growing, almost ground-cover flower and its enthusiasm for establishing itself in the gravel of a shallow running stream, justifies its inclusion. The foliage is a light, glossy green foil to the open cup-shaped yellow-centred flower bordered with white in early to late summer.

Height × spread: 15 × 15cm/6 × 6in

Soil: It will grow in moist to boggy soil (also in moist, well-drained soil).

Position: For moist areas near or in water (see above), and in sun.

Care: To start off, sow the seed in autumn or spring *in situ*.

◯ ❄❄❄

Lychnis chalcedonica: Maltese cross

With its upright habit and its cardinal red crown appearing in summer, this imposing clump-forming perennial has stout stems standing over mid-green hardy foliage. It provides an ideal companion to many other waterside broadleaf plants. The large quantity of fertile seed produced will quickly create a mass effect.

Height × spread: 1m × 30cm/3 × 1ft

Soil: It grows best in fertile, moist but well-drained soil.

Position: For moist beds and borders that are in sun.

Care: Deadhead after flowering and cut down spent growth at the end of year. Propagate by seed.

○ ❄❄❄

This clump-forming perennial with its mid-green lance-shaped leaves and its loosely upright 30cm/1ft long nodding spike composed of numerous small white flowers makes an important contribution for its late season floral display. Growing to a height of 1m/3ft and forming a dense clump at the poolside, its lush appearance can be maintained if it is given adequate moisture in full sun.

Height × spread: 1 × 1m/3 × 3ft

Soil: It grows best in fertile, moist soil which does not dry out.

Position: For moist beds and borders that are in sun or in part shade.

Care: Deadhead after flowering and cut down spent growth at the end of year. Propagate by seed or division.

◐ ❂ ❊❊❊

Lysimachia ephemerum

The linear, lance-shaped, glaucous leaves are produced from the erect stem and grow up to 15cm/6in long. The upright terminal racemes are smothered in small saucer-shaped white flowers in midsummer. These flowering spikes can be up to 37cm/15in long and are at their best in full sun or light shade. It is on the borderline of hardiness.

Height × spread: 1m × 30cm/3 × 1ft

Soil: It grows best in moist but well-drained soil, that does not dry out in the growing season.

Position: For moist beds and borders that are in sun and shelter.

Care: Deadhead after flowering and cut down spent growth at the end of year. Mulch to protect in winter. Propagate by division.

◯ | ✳✳✳ (borderline)

An adaptable, summer-flowering, perennial herb with woody stems, almost shrub-like. From the woody rootstock branched stems rise, supporting lance-shaped leaves with raised veining on the underside and slender spikes of rose pink blooms from mid to late summer. It can be propagated by seed which although viable may not come true.

Height × spread: 1m × 45cm/3 × 1½ft

Soil: It grows best in moist to boggy soil.

Position: For moist beds and borders near the water garden, that are in sun.

Care: Deadhead after flowering and cut down spent growth at the end of year. Propagate by division or cuttings, to maintain type.

○ ❄❄❄

Matteuccia struthiopteris: Ostrich fern

The stiffly upright, pale green, centre fronds surrounded by upright but more pendulous outer fronds of this fern give the impression of a dense shuttlecock form. Colonizing large areas by means of vigorous stolons, it needs careful control. It requires adequate moisture to retain its first fresh green. Good light brown autumn coloration on the maintained upright growth is a late season benefit. The spores ripen during winter. Lovely foliage plant from spring onwards.

Height × spread: 1 × 1m/3 × 3ft

Soil: It grows best in moist soil, enriched with humus, without lime.

Position: For moist beds and borders that are in part shade, though full shade is also tolerated.

Care: Tidy up spent growth at the end of year. Propagate by spores, division of the stolon in winter or stolon cuttings.

◑ LH ❄❄❄

Meconopsis × *sheldonii*: Himalayan blue poppy

One of the most beautiful of all perennials, with large, azure, saucer flowers with golden stamens in late spring and early summer. The bristly toothed green leaves form a rosette at the base. It is a hybrid of *M. grandis* and *M. betonicifolia*, and there are several outstanding forms in cultivation. The one shown is *M.* × *s.* 'Lingholm'. It is exacting about the conditions in which it will thrive and worth the best treatment.

Height × **spread:** 1.2m × 60cm/4 × 2ft

Soil: For moist, well-drained soil that is rich in humus, and neutral to acid.

Position: Grow in light shade in moist but never waterlogged beds or borders.

Care: Mulch in late winter. Water in drought. Divide every few years. Propagate by division.

◑ LH ❋❋❋

A vigorously spreading mint with showy, decorative foliage. The aromatic downy leaves are a soft grey-green and splashed, occasionally fully, with cream. Flower spikes are produced in summer consisting of tiny insignificant cream flowers. Alternatively, these can be pinched out in which case this perennial will maintain a bushier, more compact shape and its foliage will be encouraged.

Height × spread: 1 × 1m/3 × 3ft

Soil: It will grow in moist soil, including poor in which case it will be less invasive.

Position: Best in part or full shade in a moist bed where its vigour is not a problem.

Care: Cut old stems to base in late autumn. Dig out excess spread. Propagate by division.

◑ ● ❄❄❄

Mimulus × *hybridus*: Monkey flower

This cultivar of *Mimulus guttatus* × *Mimulus luteus* bears large open tubular blooms with the typical mimulus spotting in the throat. The strong colours range through cream, orange, yellow and red and these bright flowers are produced over the bushy green foliage for a prolonged period in summer. These tender perennials are usually treated as annuals.

Height × spread: 12–30 × 30cm/5in–1 × 1ft

Soil: It grows best in humus-rich, moist but not waterlogged soil.

Position: For moist beds and borders that are in sun or in part shade.

Care: Deadhead after flowering. Propagate by seed or by cuttings which are overwintered in frost-free conditions.

◯ ◑ ❄

Miscanthus floridulus: Giant Chinese silver grass

This huge, clump-forming, slowly spreading grass has strong, bamboo-like, upright stems with long, pendulous or arching, pale green leaves with silver mid ribs. It sometimes produces pyramidal panicles up to 30cm/1ft long. This plant can make an excellent screen when planted in close rows or it can be grown as a specimen plant. It is deciduous, but near evergreen in mild winters.

Height × spread: 2.4 × 1.5m/8 × 5ft

Soil: It grows best in moist but well-drained soil.

Position: For moist beds and borders that are in full sun.

Care: Cut down spent growth. Propagate by division.

| ◯ | ❋❋❋ |

Miscanthus sinensis 'Zebrinus'

This plant has a strong clump-forming habit from which grow erect, bamboo-like, cylindrical stems with a reddish tinge which mature to typical canes. The long, arching, light-green leaves are strap-like with pronounced mid ribs in white on the upper surface, which is further enhanced by pale yellow variegation in parallel blotches.

Height × spread: 1.2 × 1m/4 × 3ft

Soil: It grows best in moist but well-drained soil.

Position: For moist beds and borders that are in sun. (The variegation fades in shade.)

Care: Cut down spent growth in early spring. Propagate by division.

◯ ❄❄❄

Onoclea sensibilis: Sensitive fern

The tall sterile fronds of this fern die back at the first frost of autumn. The shorter growing fertile fronds which bear spores like small dark beads on the underside of the leaf persist through the winter. It gives an impressive golden-tan foliage effect. It is extremely vigorous and can be invasive where its chosen habitat of wet soil and full sun are provided.

Height × spread: 45cm/1¹/₂ft × indefinite spread.

Soil: It grows best in wet, humus-rich soil, ideally acidic.

Position: For wet beds and borders near the water garden, that are in part shade.

Care: Remove spent growth at the end of year. Propagate by spores, division or rhizome cuttings.

◑ | LH | ❄❄❄

Osmunda regalis: Royal fern

From early spring this complex fern uncurls its fronds which are covered in hairs. These develop into a pleasing bright green fern frond which can attain an impressive stature. Very long-lived and expanding, this spectacular waterside plant can be up to 2m/6ft high. Its autumn coloration of yellow-brown is maintained well into winter. It loves moisture and in the right setting is the first choice for architectural effect.

Height × spread: 2 × 1.5m/6 × 5ft

Soil: It grows best in humus-rich wet soil, ideally acid.

Position: For moist beds and borders near the water garden, that are in part shade.

Care: Remove spent growth at the end of year. Propagate by spores or division.

◑ LH ❄❄❄

Persicaria bistorta 'Superba'

A vigorous clump-forming perennial, with mid-green oval leaves which have prominent mid ribs giving a dense foliage cover. The flowering stems are held stiffly upright, supporting flower spikes of soft pink. It thrives in a moist soil, but unsightly wind scorch of the foliage can occur in exposed situations. It flowers from early to late summer.

Height × **spread:** 75 × 60cm/2^1/$_2$ × 2ft

Soil: It grows best in moist but well-drained soil.

Position: For moist beds and borders, protected from wind, and in sun.

Care: Deadhead after flowering and cut down spent growth at the end of year. Propagate by division.

○ | ✳✳✳

This primula with its distinctive fleshy, almost succulent, leaves provides a fresh look amongst poolside plantings. In spring to early summer the flowers are produced in a wide colour range from the palest cream to the deepest blue/purple. With close planting, dramatic effects of single colour (produced by division) or assorted colours (produced from seed) are the options.

Height × spread: 20 × 25cm/8 × 10in

Soil: It grows best in moist soil, which is gritty and well-drained, and with some leaf-mould.

Position: For moist beds and borders that are in sun, though part shade is tolerated.

Care: Deadhead after flowering and mulch with humus in late winter. Propagate by seed or division.

○ ◑ | E | ✳✳✳

Primula denticulata: Drumstick primula

Few waterside planting schemes would fail to be lifted by a bold drift of these colourful early spring-flowering primulas. The rounded, brightly coloured flowers range from whites to pinks and purples and reds and the rosettes of lance-shaped oval leaves form an effective ground cover. It makes a good show in early spring if it is planted in mass.

Height × spread: 45 × 45cm/1 $\frac{1}{2}$ × 1 $\frac{1}{2}$ft

Soil: It grows best in moist but well-drained soil, that does not dry out.

Position: For moist beds and borders in sun or part shade.

Care: Deadhead after flowering and cut down spent growth. Propagate by seed or root cuttings.

○ ◑	✲✲✲

Primula elatior: Oxlip

This semi-evergreen with its typical, scalloped, mid-green leaf presents its one-sided umbel of tubular soft yellow flowers which are up to 2.5cm/1in long, on a stout stem, during early summer. It will tolerate full sun or partial shade, providing adequate moisture is retained in the soil during the flowering season.

Height × spread: 30 × 25cm/1ft × 10in

Soil: It grows best in moist, humus-rich soil, preferably neutral to acid.

Position: For moist beds and borders in sun or part shade.

Care: Deadhead after flowering and tidy up spent growth. Propagate by seed or division when dormant.

◐ ◑ | Semi-E | LH | ❋❋❋

Primula florindae: Giant cowslip

With its rosette of broad, lance-shaped, glossy leaves of a pleasing mid-green with toothed edges, this primula produces strong upright stems, bearing a cluster of pale yellow bell-like flowers from high to late summer. Planting in partial shade with adequate moisture encourages this plant to form impressive groups. The flowers are lightly fragrant.

Height × spread: 1 × 1m/3 × 3ft

Soil: It grows best in moisture-retentive soil.

Position: For moist beds and borders near the water garden, that are in part shade.

Care: Deadhead after flowering and cut down spent growth at the end of year. Propagate by seed or division.

◑ ❄❄❄

Primula japonica: Japanese primula

This candelabra primula presents its flowers in ascending whorls in up to five or six tiers. The colours range from a deep purple through pink and white. If it is mass planted in drifts and associated with iris, hostas and other bold-leaf plantings, it gives a wonderful effect when flowering in early summer. It readily produces self-sown plantlets around its base in suitable moist and semi-shaded conditions.

Height × spread: 45 × 45cm/1 1/2 × 1 1/2ft

Soil: It grows best in moist soil, enriched with humus, which is neutral or acid.

Position: For moist beds and borders near the water garden, that are in part shade.

Care: Deadhead after flowering and tidy up spent growth. Propagate by seed or division.

◐ LH ❄❄❄

Primula 'Postford White'

This vigorous early blooming japonica primula has its flowers arranged in ascending tiers in whorls on the upright stem. It produces heavy blooms of white with a pink eye over its dark green, oval, heavily ribbed leaves. This is an early summer-flowering variety, beautiful and impressive when planted en masse.

Height × spread: 45 × 45cm/1$^1/_2$ × 1$^1/_2$ft

Soil: It grows best in moist soil, rich in humus, ideally neutral to acid.

Position: For moist beds and borders near the water garden, that are in part shade.

Care: Deadhead after flowering and tidy up spent growth. Propagate by division.

◑ LH ❄❄❄

Primula prolifera (syn. *P. helodoxa*)

This is an evergreen rosette-forming primula which displays its candelabra blooms in whorls over its dark green, finely toothed leaves. The stout flowering stems start producing multiple tiers of pale yellow blooms from early summer and providing sufficient moisture is maintained eight or nine of these tiered whorls may be presented.

Height × spread: 60 × 60cm/2 × 2ft

Soil: It grows best in reliably moist soil, rich in humus and neutral to acid.

Position: For moist beds and borders near the water garden, that are in part shade.

Care: Deadhead after flowering and tidy up spent growth. Propagate by division.

◑ E LH ❅❅❅

Primula pulverulenta

This is probably one of the finest candelabra primulas for a wet site. Its deep red blooms are arranged in whorls around the strong upright farinose (white dusted) stem in late spring and early summer. The foliage is deciduous: large, mid-green, finely toothed leaves with a distinctive pale mid rib. Drift planting creates a colourful and long-lasting waterside effect from late spring to early summer.

Height × **spread:** 60cm–1m × 30–45cm/2–3 × 1–1½ft

Soil: It grows best in reliably moist or wet soil, rich in humus, neutral or acid.

Position: For moist beds and borders near the water garden, that are in part shade.

Care: Deadhead after flowering and tidy up spent growth. Propagate by division.

◐ LH ❄❄❄

Primula sieboldii

This deciduous perennial with its pale green toothed leaves, up to 20cm/8in long, forms a compact rosette from which the trusses of reddish-violet to lilac/purple blooms with a distinctive white eye and individual petals showing a notched or frilled edge are carried. It is suitable for underplanting streamside trees or shrubs. There are also white-flowered cultivars.

Height × spread: 30 × 30–45cm/1 × 1–1¹/₂ft

Soil: It grows best in moist soil, rich in humus, neutral or acid, which does not dry out in the growing season.

Position: For moist beds and borders that are in part shade.

Care: Deadhead after flowering and tidy up spent growth. Propagate by division.

◐ LH ❋❋❋

Primula veris: Cowslip

With its golden-yellow, nodding clusters of sweetly scented bell flowers held on a stiffly upright stem, this primula will scatter its fertile seed and naturalize itself. A grassland plant, it can be increased by simply scattering seed in the autumn in the chosen location and providing adequate moisture is available, many plants will develop.

Height × spread: 20 × 20cm/8 × 8in

Soil: It grows best in moist but well-drained soil.

Position: For moist beds and borders that are in sun or part shade.

Care: Deadhead after flowering and tidy up spent growth. Propagate by seed or division.

◐ ◑ | Semi-E/E | ❊❊❊

Primula vialii

The only primrose characteristic displayed by this spectacular plant is the green, heavily ribbed, lance-shaped leaves forming an upright clump. The flowering stem produces an eye-catching small, poker-like head raised well above the foliage. The inflorescence is an attractive spike of bright scarlet re-opening to display bright pink tubular flowers. It tends to be a short-lived perennial.

Height × spread: 30–60 × 30cm/1–2 × 1ft

Soil: It grows best in moist soil, enriched with humus, which is neutral to acid.

Position: For moist beds and borders near the water garden, that are in part shade.

Care: Deadhead after flowering and tidy up spent growth. Propagate by seed or division.

◑ LH ❄❄❄

Primula vulgaris: English primrose

A neat, low-growing, clump-forming primula, native to open woodland. In a poolside situation with moist soil and adequate shade, the wrinkled leaf rosette presents on a short stem its pale yellow flower with a darker centre. It will self-seed where conditions are suitable. This plant frequently partially develops its flower buds in autumn and carries them through the winter to open in spring.

Height × spread: 20 × 20cm/8 × 8in

Soil: It grows best in moist, humus-rich soil, preferably neutral or acid.

Position: For moist beds and borders that are in sun or in part shade.

Care: Deadhead after flowering and tidy up spent growth. Propagate by seed or division.

| ○ ☽ | Semi-E/E | ❄❄❄ |

Primula vulgaris 'Alba Plena': Double primrose

There are many different cultivars of double primrose that have become widely available in recent years, in a range of colours in spring including yellow, crimson, blue-violet and also white, as illustrated. The leaves are green, wrinkled and grow in rosettes. They are not long-lived unless they are given the conditions they need including a humus-rich growing medium and regular mulching. They are formal in appearance.

Height × **spread:** 20 × 20cm/8 × 8in

Soil: For well-drained moist soil, rich in leaf-mould, ideally neutral to acid.

Position: For part or dappled shade at the front of moist but never waterlogged beds.

Care: Mulch with humus in late winter. Propagate by division.

◑ | Semi-E | ❄❄❄

Primula vulgaris subsp. *sibthorpii*

The mid-green deeply veined and sharply toothed leaves are produced in a semi-evergreen rosette. In early spring clusters of open cup-shaped, normally rosy pink but sometimes red or lilac flowers are produced, each bearing a distinctive yellow eye. This woodland variety can tolerate light shade but requires adequate moisture during the growing season.

Height × spread: 20 × 20cm/8 × 8in

Soil: It grows best in moist, humus-rich soil, ideally neutral or acid, that does not dry out in the growing season.

Position: For moist beds and borders that are in sun or in part shade.

Care: Deadhead after flowering and tidy up spent growth. Propagate by division.

◒ ◓ | Semi-E | ❄❄❄

Ranunculus ficaria **'Brazen Hussy'**: Buttercup

This tuberous perennial with a clump-forming habit has a brown/green leaf which is glossy and broadly heart-shaped, the underside being bronzed. The glossy flowers are a bright gold/yellow and are prolifically produced. This plant dies down completely after its late spring/early summer flowering and remains dormant until spring.

Height × spread: 7.5 × 30cm/3in × 1ft

Soil: It grows best in moist but well-drained soil.

Position: For moist beds and borders that are in part shade.

Care: Allow foliage and flowers to die down. Mulch in autumn. Propagate by division of tubers.

◑ ❄❄❄

Ranunculus ficaria **'Flore-pleno'**: Double lesser celandine

From tiny potato-like tubers, spreading dark green waxy round leaves not unlike those of a buttercup are produced in rosettes, followed by an attractive double celandine flower which first shows as green and matures to an eye-catching yellow with maturity. This early-flowering plant becomes dormant during summer and loses all its top growth, to be regenerated from the numerous tubers that are produced.

Height × spread: 7.5 × 30cm/3in × 1ft

Soil: It grows best in moist but well-drained soil.

Position: For moist beds and borders that are in full or semi-shade.

Care: Allow foliage and flowers to die down. Mulch in autumn. Propagate by division of tubers.

◑ ● ❊❊❊

Rheum palmatum: Ornamental rhubarb

The large rhizome produces strong leaf stalks supporting deeply lobed, almost palmate, leaves up to 1m/3ft long with a reddish underside. The towering flowering panicle bears dense tiny flowers in cream or red and can attain a height of 2m/6ft. Whilst it prefers a protected site, it is less prone to wind damage than *Gunnera manicata* and is often selected for this reason.

Height × spread: 2 × 2m/6 × 6ft

Soil: It grows best in fertile, moist soil, which is not allowed to dry out.

Position: For moist beds and borders near the water garden, in sun or part shade.

Care: Cut down spent growth. Propagate by seed or division of the rhizome.

○ ◑ | ❄❄❄

Rodgersia aesculifolia

This is a strong clump-forming plant with erect stems which have light bristle-like hairs, supporting large palmate, horse chestnut-type, green leaves which shade to bronze/green in maturity. The pyramidal flower panicles are held majestically above the architectural foliage in midsummer and are white or pink and up to 60cm/2ft tall.

Height × spread: 2 × 1m/6 × 3ft

Soil: It grows best in moist to boggy soil, that is rich in humus.

Position: For moist beds and borders that are in part shade.

Care: Deadhead after flowering and cut down spent growth at the end of year. Propagate by division in early spring.

◑ ❋❋❋

Rodgersia pinnata 'Superba'

This is a strong clump-forming plant with erect stems which have light bristle-like hairs, supporting large palmate leaves, purple-bronze in youth, which shade to green/bronze with maturity. Pyramidal flower panicles are held majestically above the architectural foliage in mid and late summer and are bright pink in colour, composed of small petalled star-shaped flowers.

Height × spread: 1.2m × 75cm/4 × 2¹/₂ft

Soil: It grows best in moist to boggy soil, that is rich in humus.

Position: For moist beds and borders that are in part shade.

Care: Deadhead after flowering and cut down spent growth at the end of year. Propagate by division in early spring.

◑ ❋❋❋

Rodgersia sambucifolia

The strong rhizome produces a dense clump of corrugated, oblong, lance-shaped, hairy leaves of a dark green, up to 75cm/2½ft tall. Over this dense foliage, tall panicles of astilbe-like flowers are produced from early to midsummer, generally white but with an occasional infusion of pink. The flower panicles are upright with nodding tips.

Height × spread: 1 × 1m/3 × 3ft

Soil: It grows best in moist to boggy soil, that is rich in humus.

Position: For moist beds and borders that are in part shade.

Care: Deadhead after flowering and cut down spent growth at the end of year. Propagate by division.

◑ | ❄❄❄

The thin iris-like foliage with a pronounced mid-rib is produced from a rooty rhizome. This slowly spreading, late-flowering, frost-hardy, waterside plant is a tremendous boost to colour in the latter part of the year. The flower spike produces creamy-white, alternate gladiolus-like blooms of an open-cup shape. Older blooms are flecked with pink.

Height × spread: 60 × 30cm/2 × 1ft

Soil: It grows best in moist, fairly fertile soil, which does not dry out but is well-drained.

Position: For moist beds and borders that are in sun.

Care: Deadhead after flowering and tidy up spent growth. Propagate by division.

○ | E | ✳✳

Schizostylis coccinea 'Sunrise'

This wonderful frost-hardy, late-flowering, clump-forming perennial has erect, narrow, almost iris-like leaves showing a distinct mid-rib. The particularly large salmon-pink flowers are produced in autumn in spikes of individual cup-shaped blooms. Flowering is usually only curtailed by the onset of winter frosts. It will self-sow in suitable conditions.

Height × spread: 60 × 30cm/2 × 1ft

Soil: It grows best in moist, fairly fertile soil, which is well-drained but does not dry out.

Position: For moist beds and borders that are in sun.

Care: Deadhead after flowering and tidy up spent growth. Propagate by division.

○ E ❋❋

Sinacalia (syn. *Senecio*) *tangutica*: Chinese groundsel

A robust perennial, spreading vigorously even in heavy clay soil, and valuable for its late season of bloom. Pyramids of starry yellow flowers are produced in autumn on tall self-supporting stems with jagged, deeply cut, dark green foliage. It looks well beside water but needs space as it is so lusty in habit and may become invasive. Not for the small garden.

Height × **spread:** 1.2 × 1.2m/4 × 4ft or more

Soil: It will grow in almost any soil, moist to boggy.

Position: For sun or part shade in beds or wilder parts by water.

Care: Excessively spreading roots may need to be dug out. Propagation by division.

○ ◑ | ✳✳✳

Sisyrinchium 'Blue Ice'

The small, grass-like, iris-shaped clumps produce startling but small pale blue/blue-violet flowers in late spring to early summer. Delicate in appearance, this plant requires moist but well-drained soil and is highly suited to the small planting scheme where it can be best appreciated. It associates well with fritillaries.

Height × **spread:** 23 × 15cm/9 × 6in

Soil: It grows best in moist but well-drained soil.

Position: For small beds that are moist but well-drained, especially in winter, and sunny.

Care: Deadhead after flowering and tidy up spent growth. Propagate by division.

| ◯ | Semi-E | ✻✻/✻✻✻ |

Sisyrinchium idahoense 'Album'

This small, clump-forming, semi-evergreen perennial produces slim, linear, iris-like, dark green leaves and in summer upright stems of white star-shaped flowers with a yellow throat. It enjoys a moist situation in summer, but needs protection from wet conditions in winter.

Height × spread: 12 × 15cm/5 × 6in

Soil: It grows best in moist but well-drained soil, that is drier in winter.

Position: For small beds and borders that are especially well-drained in winter, and sunny.

Care: Deadhead after flowering and tidy up spent growth. Propagate by division.

◑ Semi-E ❋❋/❋❋❋

Sisyrinchium striatum

This clump-forming, evergreen plant has large, flat, linear, iris-like leaves of blue-green that grow to 60cm/2ft tall. Taller flower stems, produced in early and midsummer carry numerous clusters of open, cup-shaped, pale yellow flowers. It self-sows liberally. There is a shorter growing variegated cultivar, *S. s.* 'Aunt May', the leaves of which are striped with off-white or creamy yellow.

Height × spread: 1m × 25cm/3ft × 10in

Soil: It grows best in moist but well-drained soil, drier in winter.

Position: For moist, sunny beds and borders that are well-drained in winter.

Care: Deadhead after flowering and tidy up spent growth. Propagate by seed or division.

○ E ❄❄❄

Smilacina racemosa: False Solomon's seal

Upright stems bear broadly lance-shaped, rich green leaves with parallel veining. In spring they are topped by feathery sprays of creamy white, or creamy white tinged with dusky pink, flowers, followed by berries which start cream coloured and change through green to a bright red. With all these features, this plant deserves a good shady position with adequate moisture.

Height × spread: 1m × 60cm/3 × 2ft

Soil: It grows best in moist, fertile but well-drained soil.

Position: For moist beds and borders that are in part or full shade.

Care: Cut down spent growth at the end of year. Propagate by division.

◗ ● ❋❋❋

Sorbaria tomentosa var. *angustifolia*

This false spiraea rapidly expands by the production of suckers into a dense thicket of pointed, oval, heavily toothed, mid-green leaves. The shoots are red and produce elegant loose panicles of terminal creamy white flowers. This large deciduous shrub makes a striking waterside planting which must be kept under control by removal of excess suckers.

Height × spread: 3 × 3m/10 × 10ft

Soil: It grows best in moist but well-drained soil, neutral to alkaline.

Position: For moist beds and borders near the pool, in sun or part shade.

Care: Propagate by transplanting rooted suckers in autumn.

◯ ◑ ✽✽✽

241

Telekia speciosa

With its tall brownish-red stems clothed in large, coarse, oval, upper leaves and basal leaves which are more heart-shaped, this large background plant sends up its branched flowerheads to heights of 1.5m/5ft and produces golden-yellow, daisy-like blooms in later summer. It is a vigorous plant, showy and extremely hardy.

Height × spread: 1.5 × 1m/5 × 3ft

Soil: It grows best in moist soil.

Position: For part-shady, moist beds and borders, that aren't subject to wind buffeting.

Care: Deadhead after flowering and cut down spent growth at the end of year. Propagate by seed or division.

◑ ❄❄❄

Tricyrtis formosana 'Stolonifera': Toad lily

This is a perennial for a shady situation, producing its unusual star-shaped white blooms, heavily spotted with purple-pink, with a yellow-tinged throat, from early autumn. The leaves are long, ovate, dark green and glossy with dark purple blotching and are sparingly produced. The plant expands from stolons developed from the rhizome.

Height × spread: 75 × 45cm/2^1/$_2$ × 1^1/$_2$ft

Soil: It grows best in moist soil, that is rich in humus.

Position: For shady moist beds and borders.

Care: Cut down spent growth at the end of year. Propagate by division.

◑ ● ❄❄❄

Trillium grandiflorum: Wake robin

This is a beautiful clump-forming perennial with green fleshy leaves and pure white flowers in spring which are held above the foliage. The petals are distinctly veined, developing from a cup, then opening widely with reflexed tips. It will form a most handsome plant so long as its requirement for moist soil and shade is met.

Height × spread: 45 × 30cm/1½ × 1ft

Soil: It needs moist, humus-rich soil, which is acid to neutral and well-drained.

Position: For moist beds and borders that are shady.

Care: Tidy up spent growth. Propagate by division of the rhizome after flowering.

◐ ● | LH | ❄❄❄

Trillium sessile

The leaves of this perennial are almost round and of a deep green with maroon and off-white marbling to the upper surface. In late spring burgundy or maroon flowers are produced which are stalkless and upright. This plant provides exceptional dual value, with its distinguished foliage and flowers.

Height × spread: 30 × 20cm/1ft × 8in

Soil: It needs moist, humus-rich soil, which is acid to neutral and well-drained.

Position: For moist beds and borders that are shady.

Care: Tidy up spent growth. Propagate by division of the rhizome after flowering.

◐ ● | LH | ❄❄❄

Trollius chinensis '**Golden Queen**': Globe flower

With broad, lance-shaped, much divided and toothed basal leaves and stem leaves which are smaller, the foliage provides attractive and effective clump-forming ground cover. Tall flower stems bearing many orange-stamened, golden, bowl-shaped flowers up to 5cm/2in across, are held well above the leaves in early to midsummer.

Height × **spread:** 75 × 45cm/2¹/₂ × 1¹/₂ft

Soil: It grows best in moist, fertile soil, that can be relied upon not to dry out but is well-drained.

Position: For moist beds and borders by the water, in sun or in part shade.

Care: Deadhead after flowering and cut down spent growth at the end of year. Propagate by division after flowering.

○ ◑ ❄❄❄

Uvularia grandiflora: Bellwort

The graceful, pendulous, yellow flowers of this perennial are solitary usually and bell-shaped with pointed petals. They appear in mid to late spring among the new downward-pointing, lance-shaped, mid-green leaves. It is an ideal woodland-edge or poolside plant with a need for acid conditions and part or full shade.

Height × spread: 45–75cm × 30cm/1¹/₂–2¹/₂ × 1ft

Soil: It grows best in moist, humus-rich but well-drained soil, that is acid to neutral.

Position: For moist beds and borders in shade, or woodland.

Care: Protect against damage from slugs and snails. Cut down spent growth. Propagate by division in early spring.

◐ ● | LH | ❋❋❋

Tall spikes of greenish or yellowish starry flowers are produced on this perennial in summer, similar in formation to those on the related *V. nigrum* which has striking near-black flowers, but both plants are grown less for their flowers than their splendid foliage. The pale green curving leaves, narrow at the stem and broadening out, give the appearance of being pleated.

Height × spread: 1.2m × 60cm/4 × 2ft

Soil: For rich, moist, even wet soil, which has a liberal humus-content.

Position: For part shade in moist beds or borders, which are sheltered.

Care: Mulch annually. Protect against slug damage. Propagate by division.

◑ ❋❋❋

Viola hederacea: Trailing violet, Ivy-leafed violet

In a protected site this evergreen perennial with its kidney-shaped dark-green leaves blooms prolifically. Its flowers are in shades of very pale to dark violet, or almost a cream with faint violet blotching. Expanding by short stolons, this extremely vigorous mat-forming plant makes excellent ground cover, which is enhanced by the late summer flowering. It is only frost-hardy.

Height × spread: 10 × 20cm/4 × 8in

Soil: It grows best in moist, humus-rich but well-drained soil.

Position: For moist beds and borders in full sun or part shade.

Care: Protect with a mulch during winter in cold areas. Propagate by division.

○ ◑ E ❋❋

The violet-shaped flowers have a white background, which is spectacularly and liberally dusted with violet-purple speckling. The rounded 10cm/4in long, scalloped leaves are produced from the rhizome. They are downy beneath and mid-green, and provide a good backcloth on this low-growing, clump-forming but short-lived perennial. It originates from moist meadows and rocky woodlands.

Height × **spread:** 10 × 20cm/4 × 8in

Soil: It grows best in moist but well-drained soil, which is rich in humus.

Position: For moist beds and borders in sun or in part shade.

Care: Protect against slugs. Tidy up spent growth. Propagate by division.

○ ◑ ❄❄❄

Index of Common Names

253

Index of Plants